To Mario —
 You've been
   Buddhist without
ever having become one
      formally .   Love,
WHAT COLOR   Dad
IS YOUR MIND?

Also by Thubten Chodron:

Open Heart, Clear Mind (Snow Lion Publications)
Taming the Monkey Mind (Graham Brash Publishers,
    Singapore)
Glimpse of Reality, with Alexander Berzin (Amitabha
    Buddhist Center)

WHAT COLOR IS YOUR MIND?

by

Thubten Chodron

Snow Lion Publications
Ithaca, New York USA

Snow Lion Publications
P.O. Box 6483
Ithaca, New York 14851 USA

Designed and Set in Garamond 12 on 14
by Gigantic Computing.

Printed in the United States of America

Line drawing of the Buddha by Saki Takezawa.

Library of Congress Cataloging-in-Publication Data:
Thubten Chodron, 1950-
      What color is your mind? / by Thubten Chodron. — 1st ed.
      p.   cm.
      Includes bibliographical references.
      ISBN 1-55939-015-8
      1. Buddhism—Essence, genius, nature.   I. Title
BQ4036.T48 1993
294.3—dc20   93-15016
                                         CIP

CONTENTS

THE DALAI LAMA

FOREWORD

I am happy to know about this book, WHAT COLOR IS
YOUR MIND ? by Thubten Chodron. This book is written mainly for
people wanting to understand basic Buddhist principles and how to
integrate them into their lives. It might be useful if I mention a few
words here about what should be their approach to Buddhism. In the
beginning one should remain skeptical and rely on questioning and
checking the teachings based on one's understanding. One can then
have trust and confidence in the teachings. Buddha himself
suggested this approach when he told his followers to accept his
teaching after due analysis, and not merely out of respect and faith.
Hence it is important to know that the main cause of faith is reflecting
on reasons. This promotes conviction and helps develop actual
experience. As one thinks more and more upon reasonings, one's
ascertainment increases, and this in turn, induces experience,
whereby faith becomes more firm.

I am sure that this book will be of much benefit to the readers.

October 26, 1992

INTRODUCTION

I had been in Singapore just a few days when a young man appeared at my door. "Can I ask you some questions about Buddhism?" he queried. We sat down and began to talk. Some of his questions were those also asked by Westerners new to Buddhism. Others were unique to Asians who had grown up in societies where Buddhism and the old folk religions were often mixed, at least in the minds of the general population. As I began teaching in Singapore, I noticed that many people had the same questions.

Soon thereafter, another man came to see me, and in the course of our discussion he said, "We need to hear about the Buddha's teachings in everyday English, a clear explanation without a lot of Pali and Sanskrit terms that we don't understand. Why not write a book with some of your talks? I'd be happy to help you."

The idea for this book came from these two people—Lee Siew Cheung and Robert Gwee. It was initially printed privately in Singapore by Amitabha Buddhist Centre in 1988 and was entitled *I Wonder Why*. As people read it, they sent me more questions. I have included these in the present edition. The second section of the book, "Working with Anger," deals with a topic that is timely in both the East and West. It is a combination of two talks I gave on the subject: one at Evergreen Buddhist Association in Kirkland, Washington, in 1989, and the other at a conference entitled "Buddhism and Psychology" at the University of Washington in Seattle, in 1992.

Because the greater part of this book consists of questions and answers, I thought to make the title a question as well. But "What color is your mind?" has no answer, because our minds, as distinct from our brains, don't have color or shape. They are that part of us that perceives, feels and thinks. Our minds experience happiness and pain; they motivate what we say and do; they can span the continuum from confusion to enlightenment. The search to understand our own minds, to be at peace within ourselves, is the most valuable one we can go on.

This book is designed for people who are just becoming interested in Buddhism as well as those who have studied or practiced it for years but are still unclear about some points. It seems that the way some of the initial material on Buddhism was translated decades ago has led to some misinterpretations even among those who teach Buddhism at the high school and college levels. I hope that this small book will help them and their students.

You can read the book from cover to cover or go directly to the sections that interest you. This book isn't designed to be a comprehensive introduction to Buddhism, but to clarify points, provide Buddhist perspectives on modern issues and stimulate the curiosity and questioning minds of the readers.

My deepest respect and gratitude are offered to the Buddhas. I would like to thank all of my teachers, in particular His Holiness the Dalai Lama, Ven. Tsenzhab Serkong Rinpoche and Ven. Zopa Rinpoche, for their teachings and guidance. I deeply appreciate the members of Amitabha Buddhist Center in Singapore and Dharma Friendship Foundation in Seattle for their inspiration and help in writing this book. Special thanks go to Monica Faulkner for her help in editing the manuscript and to Cindy Loth for proofreading it. All errors are my own.

Some technical notes: "He" and "she" are used interchangeably for the third person pronoun. "Mind," "mindstream," and "consciousness" are used interchangeably to refer to the part of us that perceives and experiences. This includes what we call "heart" in the West; in Buddhism, one word encompasses the meaning of heart and mind. "The Buddha" refers to the historical Buddha, Shakyamuni, who lived in India over 2,500 years ago. "Buddhas" refers to all enlightened beings, of whom Shakyamuni is one.

I have tried to define Buddhist terms as they arise in the text, and there is a glossary at the end of the book that you can also use.

Thubten Chodron
Seattle, U.S.A.
1993

Part One
WHAT COLOR IS YOUR MIND?

Chapter 1

THE ESSENCE OF BUDDHISM

What is the essence of the Buddha's teachings?

Simply speaking, it is to avoid harming others and to help them as much as possible. Another way of expressing this is, "Abandon negative action; create perfect virtue; subdue your own mind. This is the teaching of the Buddha." By abandoning negative actions, such as hurting others, and destructive motivations, such as anger, attachment and closed-mindedness, we stop harming ourselves and others. By creating perfect virtue, we develop beneficial attitudes, such as impartial love and compassion, and act constructively. By subduing our minds and understanding reality, we leave behind all false projections, thus making ourselves calm and peaceful.

The essence of the Buddha's teachings is also contained in the three principles of the path: the determination to be free, the altruistic intention and the wisdom realizing the lack of fantasized ways of existence. Initially, we must have the determination to be free from the confusion of our problems and their causes. Then we'll see that other people also have problems, and with love and compassion we'll develop an altruistic intention to become a Buddha so that we will be capable of helping others effectively. To do this, we must develop the wisdom which understands the real nature of ourselves and other phenomena and thus eliminates all false projections.

What are the Three Jewels? What does it mean to take refuge in them?

The Three Jewels are the Buddha, Dharma and Sangha. A Buddha is one who has purified all the defilements of the mind—the disturbing attitudes, the imprints of the actions motivated by them, and the stains of these disturbing attitudes. A Buddha has also developed all good qualities, such as impartial love and compassion, profound wisdom and skillful means of guiding others. The Dharma is the preventive measures that keep us from problems and suffering. This includes the teachings of the Buddha and the beneficial mental states that practicing the teachings leads to. The Sangha are those beings who have direct nonconceptual understanding of the lack of fantasized ways of existence. *Sangha* can also refer to the community of ordained people who practice Buddha's teachings.

What is the goal of the Buddhist path?

It is to discover a state of lasting happiness for both ourselves and others by freeing ourselves from cyclic existence, the cycle of constantly recurring problems that we experience at present. Under the influence of ignorance, disturbing attitudes and actions, we are born and die, experiencing various problems during our lives. Although all of us want to be happy and we try hard to get the things that will make us happy, no one is totally satisfied with his or her life. And although we all want to be free from difficulties, problems come our way without our even trying. People may have many good things going for them in their lives, but when we talk with them for more than five minutes, they start telling us their problems. Those of us who are in this situation, who aren't yet Buddhas, are called "sentient beings."

The root cause of cyclic existence is ignorance: we don't understand who we are, how we exist or how other phenomena exist. Unaware of our own ignorance, we project fantasized ways of existing onto ourselves and others, thinking that everyone and everything has some inherent nature and exists independently, in and of itself. This gives rise to attachment, an attitude that exaggerates the good qualities of people and things or superimposes good qualities that aren't there and then clings to those people or things, thinking they will bring us real happiness. When things don't work out as we expected or wished they would, or when something interferes with our happiness, we become angry. These three basic disturbing attitudes—ignorance, attachment and anger—give rise to a host of other ones, such as jealousy, pride and resentment. These attitudes then motivate us to act, speak or think. Such actions (karma) leave imprints on our mindstreams and these imprints then influence what we'll experience in the future.

We are liberated from the cycle of rebirth by generating the wisdom realizing "emptiness" or "selflessness." This wisdom is a profound understanding of the lack of fantasized ways of existing: the lack of a solid, independent self. It eliminates all ignorance, wrong conceptions and disturbing attitudes, thus putting a stop to all misinformed or contaminated actions. The state of being liberated is called nirvana or liberation. All beings have the potential to attain liberation, a state of lasting happiness.

The Buddha summarized the process of going from confusion to enlightenment in the four noble truths. First, we have unsatisfactory experiences in life; second, these experiences have causes; third, it is possible to remove these causes and their consequent difficulties, thus arriving at a state of lasting happiness; and fourth, there is a path or method to do this.

How do we relate to the Three Jewels? What does it mean to take refuge in them?

Our relationship to the Three Jewels is analogous to a person who is ill seeking help from a doctor, medicine and a nurse. We suffer from various unsatisfactory circumstances in our lives. The Buddha is like a doctor who correctly diagnoses the cause of our problems and prescribes the appropriate medicine. The Dharma is our real refuge, the medicine that cures our problems and their causes. By helping us along the path, the Sangha is like the nurse who assists us in taking the medicine.

Taking refuge means relying wholeheartedly on the Three Jewels to inspire and guide us toward a constructive and beneficial direction in our lives. Taking refuge does not mean passively hiding under the protection of the Buddha, Dharma and Sangha. Rather, it is an active process of moving in the direction they show and thus improving the quality of our life.

When people take refuge, they clarify to themselves what direction they're taking in life, who is guiding them, and who their companions are on the path. This eliminates the indecision and confusion arising from uncertainty about their spiritual path. Some people window-shop for spirituality: Monday they use crystals, Tuesday they do channeling, Wednesday they do Hindu meditation, Thursday they do Hatha Yoga, Friday they have holistic healing, Saturday they do Buddhist meditation, and Sunday they use Tarot cards. They learn a lot about many things, but their attachment, anger and closed-mindedness don't change much. Taking refuge is making a clear decision about what one's principal path is. However, it's possible to practice the Buddha's teachings and to benefit from them without taking refuge or becoming a Buddhist.

Must we be a Buddhist to practice what the Buddha taught?

No. The Buddha gave a wide variety of instructions, and if some of them help us live better, to solve our problems and become kinder, then we're free to practice them. There's no need to call ourselves Buddhists or to accept a dogma. The purpose of the teachings is to benefit us, and if putting some of them into practice helps us live more peacefully with ourselves and others, that's what's important.

Chapter 2

THE BUDDHA

Who is the Buddha? If he is just a man, how can he help us?

There are many ways to describe who the Buddha is. These various perspectives have their sources in the Buddha's teachings. One is the historical Buddha, a human being who lived 2,500 years ago and who cleansed his mind of all defilements and developed all of his potential. Any being who does likewise is also considered a Buddha, for there are many Buddhas, not just one. Another way is to understand a particular Buddha or Buddhist deity as the enlightened minds manifesting in a certain physical aspect in order to communicate with us. Yet another way is to see the Buddha or any of the enlightened Buddhist deities as the appearance of the future Buddha that we will become once we have completely cleansed our minds of defilements and developed all of our potential. Let's examine each of these ways in more depth.

The Historical Buddha

The historical Buddha Shakyamuni was born as Prince Siddhartha Gautama in an area near the present border between India and Nepal. He had all that life could offer: material possessions, a loving family, fame, reputation and power. However, he gradually came to understand that although those things bring temporary, worldly happiness, they are incapable of bringing lasting happiness. Thus he left the princely environment and became an ascetic searching for truth. After six years of severe physical austerity, he realized that extreme self-denial was not the path to ultimate happiness. At this point, he sat under the bodhi tree, and in deep meditation completely purified his mind of all wrong conceptions and defilements and perfected all of his potential and good qualities. He then proceeded with great compassion, wisdom and skill to give teachings, thus enabling others to gradually purify their minds, develop their potential, and attain the same realizations and state of happiness that he had. Thus, the word *Buddha* means "the awakened one," one who has purified and developed his or her mind completely.

How can such a person save us from our problems and pain? The Buddha can't pull the disturbing attitudes of ignorance, anger and attachment from our minds in the same way as a thorn can be extracted from our foot. Nor can the Buddha wash away our defilements with water, or pour realizations into our minds. The Buddha has impartial compassion for all sentient beings and cherishes us more than himself, so if our sufferings could have been eliminated by his action, the Buddha would have done so.

However, our experience of happiness and pain depends on our minds. It depends on whether or not we assume the responsibility to subdue our disturbing attitudes and contaminated actions (*karma*). The Buddha showed the method to do this, the method that he himself used to go from the state of an ordinary confused being, the way we are now, to the state of total purification and growth, or Buddhahood. It's up to us to practice this method and transform our own minds. Shakyamuni Buddha is someone who did what we want to do—he reached a state of lasting happiness. His example and his teachings indicate how we can do the same. But the Buddha can't control our minds, only we can do that. Our enlightenment depends not only on the Buddha showing us the way, but also on our own efforts to follow it.

To use an analogy, suppose we want to go to London. First we find out if such a place called London actually exists. Then we look for someone who has been there and who has the knowledge, capability and willingness to give us all of the travel information. It would be foolish to follow someone who had never been there, because that person could unwittingly give us mistaken information. Likewise, the Buddha has attained enlightenment; he has the wisdom, compassion and skill to show us the path. It would be silly to entrust ourselves to a guide who had not reached the enlightened state him- or herself.

Our travel guide can give us information about what to take with on our trip and what to leave behind. He or she can tell us how to change planes, how to recognize the various places we'll pass through, what dangers we could encounter along the way and so forth. Similarly, the Buddha has described the various levels of the paths and stages, how to progress from one to the next, what qualities to take with us and develop, and which ones to leave behind. However, a travel guide can't force us to make the journey—he or she can only indicate the way. We have to go to the airport ourselves and get on the plane. Likewise, the Buddha can't force us to practice the path. He gives the teachings and shows by his example how to do it, but we have to do it ourselves.

The Buddhas As Manifestations

The second way to think of the Buddhas is as manifestations of enlightened minds in physical forms, that is, as Buddhist deities. Buddhas are omniscient in that they perceive all existent phenomena as clearly as we can see the palm of our hand. They achieved this ability by fully developing their wisdom and compassion, thus eliminating all obscurations. But we can't communicate directly with the Buddhas' omniscient minds because our minds are obscured. For the Buddhas to fulfill their most heartfelt wish to lead all beings to enlightenment, they must communicate with us, and to do so, they assume physical forms. In this way, we can think of Shakyamuni Buddha as a being who was already enlightened, and who appeared in the aspect of a prince in order to teach us.

But if Shakyamuni was already enlightened, how can he take rebirth? He didn't take rebirth under the control of disturbing attitudes and contaminated actions (karma) as ordinary beings do, because he had already eliminated these defilements from his mind. However, he was able to appear on this earth by the power of compassion. Similarly, high-level bodhisattvas—beings who have the constant and intense wish to become a Buddha in order to benefit others—can voluntarily take rebirth, not out of ignorance as ordinary beings do, but out of compassion.

When thinking of the Buddha as a manifestation, don't emphasize the Buddha as a personality. Rather, concentrate on the qualities of the omniscient minds appearing in the form of a person. This is a more abstract way of understanding the Buddha, so it takes more effort on our part to think in this way and to understand.

In the same way, the various enlightened Buddhist deities can be seen as manifestations of the qualities of omniscient minds. Why are there so many deities if all the beings who have attained enlightenment have the same realizations? This is because each physical appearance emphasizes and communicates with different aspects of our personality. This demonstrates the Buddhas' skillful means, their ability to guide others according to their disposition. For example, Avalokiteshvara (Kuan Yin, Chenresig, Kannon) is the manifestation of the compassion of all the Buddhas. Although possessing all the compassion and wisdom of any Buddha, Avalokiteshvara's particular manifestation emphasizes compassion. Enlightened compassion can't be seen with the eyes, but if it were to appear in physical form, what would it look like?

In the same way that artists express themselves symbolically through images, the Buddhas express their compassion symbolically by appearing in the form of Avalokiteshvara. In some drawings, Avalokiteshvara is white and has a thousand arms. The white color emphasizes purity, in this case the purification of selfishness through compassion. The thousand arms, each with an eye in its palm, expresses how impartial compassion looks upon all beings and is willing to reach out to help them. By body language alone, Avalokiteshvara demonstrates compassion. By visualizing compassion in this physical aspect, we can communicate with compassion in a nonverbal and symbolic way.

The deity Manjushri is the manifestation of the wisdom of all the Buddhas. Manjushri has the same realizations as all the Buddhas. In the Tibetan tradition Manjushri is depicted as yellow in color, holding a flaming sword and a lotus flower upon which rests the *Perfection of Wisdom Sutra*. This physical form is symbolic of inner realizations. The color yellow represents wisdom, which illuminates the mind just as golden rays of the sun light up the earth. The sword too represents wisdom in its function of cutting ignorance. Holding the *Perfection of Wisdom Sutra* indicates that to develop wisdom, we must study, contemplate and meditate on the meanings contained in this sutra. By visualizing and meditating on Manjushri, we can attain the qualities of a Buddha, especially wisdom.

These examples help us to understand why there are so many deities. Each emphasizes a particular aspect of the enlightened qualities and communicates that aspect to us symbolically. That does not mean, however, that there is no such being as Avalokiteshvara. On one level, we can understand the Buddha of Compassion to be a person residing in a certain Pure Land, a place where all conditions are conducive for spiritual growth. On another level, we can see Avalokiteshvara as a manifestation of compassion in a physical form. In Tibet Avalokiteshvara is depicted in a male form and in China in a female form. This isn't because enlightened beings can't make up their minds! An enlightened mind is actually beyond being male or female. The various physical forms are simply appearances to communicate with us ordinary beings who are so involved in forms. An enlightened being can appear in a wide variety of bodies. If it's more effective to appear in a female form for people of one culture and a male form for people of another, an enlightened being will do that.

The nature of these various manifestations is the same: the omniscient mind of wisdom and compassion. All of the Buddhas and deities are not separate beings in the same way that an apple and an orange are separate fruits. Rather, they all have the same nature; they only appear in different external forms in order to communicate with us in different ways. From one lump of clay, someone can make a pot, a vase, a plate, or a figurine. The nature of all of them is the same—clay—yet they perform different functions according to how the clay is shaped. In the same way, the nature of all the Buddhas and deities is the omniscient mind of wisdom and compassion. This appears in a variety of forms in order to perform various functions. Thus, when we want to develop compassion, we emphasize meditation on Avalokiteshvara; when our mind is dull and sluggish, we emphasize the practice of Manjushri, the Buddha of Wisdom. These Buddhas all have the same realizations, yet each one has his or her specialty.

The Buddha That We Will Become

The third way to understand the Buddha is as the appearance of our own Buddha nature in its fully developed form. All beings have the potential to become Buddhas, for all of our minds are innately pure. At the present they are clouded by disturbing attitudes (*klesa*) and contaminated actions (*karma*). Through constant practice, we can remove these defilements from our mind streams and nourish the seeds of the beautiful potentials we have. Thus each of us can become a Buddha when this process of purification and growth is completed. This is a unique feature of Buddhism, for most other religions say there is an unbridgeable gap between the divine being and the human being. However, the Buddha said that each being has the potential to become fully enlightened. It is only a matter of practicing the path and creating the causes to reach enlightenment. Thus there are many beings who have already become Buddhas, and we can become one as well.

When we visualize the Buddha or a deity and think of him or her as the future Buddha that we will become, we are imagining our now latent Buddha nature in its completely developed form. We're thinking of the future, when we will have completed the path to enlightenment. By imagining the future in the present, we reaffirm our own latent goodness. The future Buddha we will become is the real protection from our suffering, because by becoming this Buddha, we'll have eliminated the causes for our present unsatisfactory conditions.

These different ways of understanding the Buddha are progressively more difficult to understand. We may not grasp them immediately. That's all right. Various interpretations are explained because people have different ways of understanding. We aren't expected to all think in the same way or to understand everything at once.

If there are people alive today who have attained Buddhahood, why don't they tell us who they are and demonstrate their clairvoyant powers to generate faith in others? Why do the great masters all deny having spiritual realizations?

One of the principal qualities of an enlightened being is humility. It would be out of character for Buddhas to boast about their attainments and to egotistically gather disciples. By their genuine respect for all beings and their willingness to learn from everyone, great spiritual masters set a good example for us. We ordinary beings tend to show off our qualities and even brag about talents and achievements that aren't ours. Advanced practitioners are the opposite: they remain humble.

The Buddha forbade his followers to display their clairvoyant or miraculous powers unless it was absolutely necessary, and they are not allowed to talk about them. There are several reasons for this. If one has clairvoyant powers and displays them, one's pride could increase and this would be detrimental to one's practice. Also, others might get superstitious and think that clairvoyant powers are the goal of the path. In fact, they are a side effect and are useful only if one has the proper motivation of impartial loving-kindness for all. In addition, if a Buddha, with a body made of radiant light, suddenly appeared on the street, people would be so shocked that they couldn't pay attention to that Buddha's teachings. It's more skillful for those who have attained high levels of the path to appear in ordinary form. We may notice that they have exceptional qualities, but the fact that they look just like us allows us to feel closer to them. It gives us the confidence that we too can develop enlightened qualities.

What does faith mean in Buddhism? Can we receive grace from the Buddhas?

Buddhism encourages us to learn the Buddha's teachings and to try them out, and in that way develop faith or confidence in them. There are three types of confidence in Buddhism:

1. *Pure or admiring confidence.* We admire the qualities of the Buddha, Dharma and Sangha by knowing their qualities.

2. *Aspiring confidence.* By recognizing the qualities of the Three Jewels, we aspire to become like them.

3. *Confidence from conviction.* By examining the teachings and applying them in our lives, we develop the conviction that they are effective.

Buddhism doesn't use the word *grace* per se, but there is a similar concept, which is translated as receiving the inspiration or the blessings of the Three Jewels. This means that our minds are transformed as a result not only of the influence of the Three Jewels, but also as a result of our practice and openness.

Chapter 3

IMPERMANENCE AND SUFFERING

Buddhism talks a lot about impermanence, death and suffering. Isn't such an approach to life unhealthy and pessimistic?

The word *suffering* isn't an accurate translation of the Pali *dukkha* or Sanskrit *duhkha*. Duhkha has the connotation of unsatisfactory experiences; it means that everything isn't completely wonderful in our lives. While most of us don't feel we are suffering all the time, we would agree that not everything in our lives is perfect. Even when we're relatively happy, there's no guarantee that things will continue to go well. One small event can change our entire experience. This is what is meant by unsatisfactory experiences, duhkha or suffering. The Buddha merely described our present situation; therefore he was being realistic, not pessimistic. His motivation for describing this was to help us seek the means to free ourselves from it.

The purpose of contemplating impermanence, death and unsatisfactory experiences isn't to become depressed and have the joy taken out of life. Rather, the purpose is to rid ourselves of attachment and false expectations. If we become emotionally afraid or depressed when thinking about these things, then we aren't contemplating them correctly. Meditating on these subjects should make our minds calm and lucid because it decreases our clinging attachment and the confusion it causes in our lives.

At present, our minds are easily overwhelmed by the false projections of attachment. We see people and objects in an unrealistic way. Things are changing moment by moment but they appear to us to be constant and unchanging. That's why we are upset when they break. We may say, "All these things are impermanent," but our words aren't consistent with our innate view, which considers our body and other things to be unchanging. Our unrealistic conception causes us pain, because we have expectations of things and people that can't be fulfilled. Our loved ones can't live forever; a relationship doesn't remain the same; the new car won't always be the shiny model just off the showroom floor. Thus, we are perpetually disappointed when we must part with people we care for, when our possessions break, when our body becomes weak or old. If we had a more realistic view of these things and accepted their impermanence—not just with our words but with our heart—then such disappointment would not come.

Contemplating impermanence and death also eliminates many of the useless worries that prevent us from being happy and relaxed. Ordinarily, we become upset when we are criticized or insulted: we are angry when our possessions are stolen; we feel jealous if someone else gets the promotion we wanted; we are proud of our looks or athletic ability. All of these attitudes are disturbing emotions that leave harmful imprints on our mindstreams and bring us problems in our future lives as well as in this life. However, if we contemplate the transient nature of these things, if we remember that our life will end and that none of these things can accompany us at death, then we will stop exaggerating their importance. They will no longer be so problematic for us.

That doesn't mean that we become apathetic toward the people and things around us. On the contrary, by eliminating the wrong conception of permanence and the disturbing attitudes that stem from it, our minds will become clearer and we'll be able to enjoy things for what they are. We'll live more in the present, appreciating things as they are now, without fantasies about what they should be or might become. We'll worry less about small matters, and will be less distracted when we meditate. We'll become less touchy about how others treat us. By reflecting on impermanence and unsatisfactory experiences, we can deal better with all the unpleasant events that occur because we're still in the cycle of constantly recurring problems. In short, by correctly contemplating these truths, our mental state will become healthier.

Why is there suffering? How can we stop it?

Unsatisfactory experiences occur simply because the causes for them exist. One cause is the disturbing attitudes, such as ignorance, attachment and anger. The other is the actions we engage in, such as killing, stealing and lying, which are motivated by the disturbing attitudes. By developing the wisdom realizing selflessness, we'll eliminate the disturbing attitudes and their resultant actions, thus stopping the causes of our problems. Then the painful results can't follow, and instead, we'll abide in a state of lasting happiness or nirvana. In the meantime, before we generate that wisdom, we can do purification practices to prevent the results of our previous destructive actions. The Buddha also taught many techniques for mentally transforming difficult circumstances into the path to enlightenment. We can learn about these and practice them when we have problems.

Do we have to suffer to attain liberation (nirvana)? Must we renounce the world to become a Buddha?

Practicing Buddha's teachings brings happiness, not pain. The spiritual path itself isn't painful, and there is no special virtue in suffering. We already have enough problems, so there's no sense in causing ourselves more in the name of practicing religion. However, that doesn't mean that we won't have any problems while practicing the Dharma. While we're on the path, previous destructive actions that haven't yet been purified may ripen and bring problems. When this happens, we can transform the situation into the path to enlightenment through using the various techniques the Buddha taught. Sometimes our anger, attachment or jealousy may arise strongly and be very disquieting when we're trying to practice. This happens because our disturbing attitudes haven't yet been eliminated. After all, we don't become Buddhas after practicing the Dharma for just a short time! We can apply the Buddha's teachings to subdue these unpleasant emotions, while being patient with ourselves and recognizing that purifying our minds takes time.

Although the English word *renunciation* is often used in Buddhist translations, it doesn't convey the real meaning. It's more accurate to say that we must develop the determination to be free from cyclic existence and to become liberated. We don't need to renounce people and things. Rather, we need to give up our clinging attachment to them. There is nothing inherently wrong with the world; the real problem lies in our disturbing attitudes. For example, money isn't the problem. It's merely sheets of paper. However, our clinging to and craving for money cause big problems. These erroneous and harmful attitudes are to be given up. Of course, if we're very attached to something, it's a good idea to distance ourselves from it for a while to calm our clinging. If we're attached to ice cream, it's very hard not to eat it if we go to an ice cream parlor! Later, when we've developed a more balanced and altruistic motivation, we can use the former objects of attachment for the benefit of others.

Buddhism talks about accepting our suffering and also about freeing ourselves from suffering. Are these contradictory?

No. Accepting our difficulties doesn't mean becoming apathetic and resigned to suffering. Rather, our experience at a particular moment—whatever it is—is the reality of that moment. When we refuse to accept this, we find ourselves in conflict either internally or with our environment. On the other hand, we can accept our present unhappiness and still work to free ourselves from future unsatisfactory experiences. In fact, once we have developed the determination to be free from cyclic existence, the method for doing this is to accept reality for what it is. For example, if we accept the transient nature of our world, we'll cease trying to fixate and control things that are uncontrollable. We'll be at peace with whatever life presents and simultaneously work for the benefit of others with an altruistic aspiration that appreciates every being's potential to transcend suffering and be enlightened.

Chapter 4

SELFLESSNESS AND EMPTINESS

Do "selflessness" and "emptiness" mean the same thing? What is the advantage of realizing selflessness or emptiness?

In general, these two terms are synonymous, although when studying philosophy in depth, there are differences between them. By realizing emptiness, we'll be able to cleanse our minds of all defilements and obscurations. At the moment, our minds are obscured by ignorance: the way we perceive and grasp ourselves and other phenomena to exist is not the way they really exist. It's similar to people who wear sunglasses all the time. Everything they see appears dark and they think that's the way things are. But if they took off their sunglasses they'd find that things actually exist in a different way.

Another analogy to the view of ignorance is people who watch a movie and think that the people on the screen are real. The viewers become very emotional and involved in the fate of the characters. Being attached to the hero, they are antagonistic to the characters who threaten him. The audience may even cry out, cringe, or jump up from their seats when the hero is harmed. In fact, these reactions are out of proportion, for there are no real people on the screen at all. They are only projections that are dependent on causes and conditions such as the film, the film projector and the screen. Realizing emptiness is analogous to understanding that the movie is empty of real people. However, the appearance of the characters does exist, dependent on the film, screen and so forth. If we understand this, we can still enjoy the film, but we no longer go up and down emotionally as the hero experiences various events.

By generating the wisdom that directly realizes emptiness, we'll perceive the mode in which we and all other phenomena exist: they are empty of our fantasized projections on them—especially the projection of inherent existence. Having this wisdom realizing reality, we'll gradually free ourselves from the bonds of the ignorance that misconceives reality. As we familiarize ourselves with emptiness, we'll gradually eliminate all ignorance, anger, attachment, pride, jealousy, and other disturbing attitudes from our mind. By doing so, we'll cease to create the destructive actions motivated by them. Freed from ignorance, disturbing attitudes and the actions motivated by them, we'll be liberated from the causes of our problems, and thus the problems also will cease. In other words, the wisdom realizing emptiness is the true path to happiness.

What does it mean to say, "All persons and phenomena are empty of true or inherent existence?"

It means that all persons (such as you and I) and all other phenomena (tables, etc.) are empty of our fantasized projections on them. One of the principal deceptive qualities that we project onto persons and phenomena is that they are inherently existent, that is, that they exist without depending on causes and conditions, the parts of which they are made, and the consciousness that conceives them and gives them a name. Thus, in our ordinary view, things appear to have some true or inherent nature, as if they were really there, as if we could find these real, independent entities if we searched for them. They appear to be there, independent of the causes and conditions that created them, independent of the parts of which they are made, and independent of the mind that conceives and gives them a name. This is the appearance of true or inherent existence and our minds grasp it as real.

However, when we examine analytically if things exist in this independent way as they superficially appear to, we find that they do not. They are empty of our fantasized projections onto them. Still, they do exist, but they exist dependently, for they rely on causes and conditions, on the parts which compose them, and on the mind that conceives them and gives them a name.

If all people and phenomena are selfless or empty, does that mean that nothing exists?

No, phenomena and people still exist. After all, I am still here typing and you are still reading! Emptiness is not the same as nihilism. Rather, people and phenomena are empty of our fantasized projections upon them. They lack what our wrong conceptions attribute to them. They do not exist in the way they appear to us at present, but they do exist: they don't exist independently, but they do dependently exist. For example, someone who is wearing sunglasses sees dark trees. In fact, there are no dark trees. However, we can't say there are no trees at all. There are trees; they just don't exist in the way they appear to the person wearing sunglasses.

Is realizing emptiness the same as having a blank mind free from all thoughts?

No. When emptiness is realized directly, the mind is also free from thoughts and concepts. However, just removing all thoughts from our minds—peaceful though it may be—isn't realizing emptiness. After all, cows' minds are pretty blank but they don't realize emptiness! Understanding emptiness involves understanding what things are empty of—inherent or independent existence—and then realizing that inherent existence is a hallucination which has never existed at all.

Sometimes people feel that their lives are empty. Is this the same emptiness spoken of by the Buddha?

No. In everyday language, we say people feel empty when they lack goals or close relationships with others or lack a sense of meaning in their lives. This is a lack of external relationships, clear personal goals or internal tranquility. It is resolved by developing self-confidence, setting priorities in life and letting go of unrealistic expectations of themselves and others.

On the other hand, the emptiness that the Buddha spoke of deals with the mode of existence of phenomena: it is the lack of fantasized ways of existing. Understanding this emptiness leads to a feeling of fullness and meaning in our lives because we'll be free from all restricting misconceptions and disturbing emotions. This emptiness is realized through studying, thinking about and meditating on the Buddha's teachings.

Psychologists tell us that a strong sense of self is essential for psychological health. But it seems Buddhism says there is no self. How can we reconcile these two views?

When psychologists speak of a sense of self, they're referring to the feeling of being an efficacious person, someone who is self-confident and can act in the world. Buddhists agree that such a sense of self is both realistic and necessary. However, the sense of self that Buddhism says is unrealistic is that of a solid, unchanging, independent "I." Such a self never has and never will exist. To understand this is to realize emptiness.

What is the best way to realize the emptiness of inherent existence?

This realization is difficult to gain and is attained at advanced stages of the path, so we must develop our understanding slowly. The path to liberation and enlightenment is a gradual one that is practiced in steps. First we train in the elementary aspects of the path, such as impermanence, refuge, the determination to be free from cyclic existence, love and compassion. Then we listen to teachings on emptiness from knowledgeable and compassionate spiritual mentors. As we think about and discuss these teachings, our understanding will become clearer. Once we have a clear idea of the subject, we can begin to integrate it into our minds through meditation.

Chapter 5

SCIENCE, REBIRTH AND CREATION

What is the relationship between Buddhism and science?

They have many points in common: for example, both depend on logic and investigation to ascertain the nature of phenomena. Both discourage blind belief and encourage free inquiry on the part of the student. Buddhism doesn't contradict current scientific theories about the origin of this universe or the physical evolution of the human species. In fact, His Holiness the Dalai Lama has said that if scientific findings contradict what is written in Buddhist scriptures, then Buddhists must accept that new information. However, if science cannot actively disprove what is stated in the scriptures, there is no need to abandon that concept. For example, although scientists have not yet been able to prove the existence of rebirth, neither have they been able to disprove it.

Both science and Buddhism rely upon cause and effect to explain how things function: science investigates cause and effect as it functions in the physical, material world, whereas Buddhism explores it in terms of the mind.

Both emphasize the dependent nature of phenomena. Things rely on causes, the parts of which they are made, and the consciousness that observes and labels them. Quantum physicists are becoming increasingly aware of the latter when doing experiments. They recognize that the experimenter isn't an independent entity who objectively observes external phenomena. Rather, he or she influences the results of an experiment simply by observing it. This relates to the Buddha's teaching on the emptiness of inherent existence, which emphasizes the dependent relationship between consciousness and the objects it perceives.

Many scientists believe it is impossible to find the smallest partless particles from which all matter is created. Buddhism agrees that isolating the smallest independent particles is impossible. Yet at meetings with scientists, His Holiness the Dalai Lama has mentioned dependently existing "space particles," which contain the potentials of all other elements in the universe. What precisely is meant by "space particles" and how they relate to scientific theories and discoveries needs to be explored further.

The Buddhist concept of dependent arising can also be applied in the area of neurology, where it's evident that perception isn't an isolated phenomenon, but the coming together of various factors. Just as scientists say it's impossible to set apart one particular cell or chemical-electrical process that constitutes perception, so too Buddhists say that cognition is dependent on a variety of factors, none of which constitute perception in and of themselves.

More scientists are becoming interested in Buddhism, and some Buddhist scholars are learning about modern science. His Holiness the Dalai Lama has attended several conferences with scientists that have been fruitful for everyone concerned. It is hoped that such exchange of ideas will increase in the future.

What is rebirth?

Rebirth refers to a person's mind taking one body after another. Our body and our mind are separate entities. Our body is matter and is made of atoms. Our mind refers to all of our emotional and cognitive experiences, and is formless. The word "mind" in a Buddhist sense also includes what in English is referred to as heart, as in "he has a kind heart." While we are alive, the body and mind are linked, but at death they separate. The body becomes a corpse, and the mind continues on to take another body. To emphasize the continuity of consciousness, we also use the word "mindstream" to refer to our mind. Each person has a separate mind or mindstream.

How did our mind begin? Who or what created it?

Each moment of mind is a continuation of the previous moment. Who we are and what we think and feel depends on who we were yesterday. Our present mind is a continuation of yesterday's mind. That is why we can remember what happened to us in the past. One moment of our mind was caused by the previous moment of our mind. This continuity can be traced back to childhood and even to when we were a fetus in our mother's womb. Even before the time of conception, our mindstream existed: its previous moments were linked to another body.

Our mind has no beginning. Who said there had to be a beginning? The continuity of our mind is infinite. This may be difficult to grasp initially, but if we use the example of a number line, it becomes easier. From the zero position, looking left, there is no first negative number, and looking right, there is no last, highest number. One more can always be added on. In the same way, our mindstream has no beginning and no end. We all have had an infinite number of past rebirths, and our mind will continue to exist infinitely. However, by purifying our mindstream, we can make our future existence better than our present one.

In fact, it would be impossible for our mindstream to have a beginning. Because each moment of mind is caused by its previous moment, if there were a beginning, then either the first moment of mind had no cause or it was caused by something other than a previous moment of mind. But both of those alternatives are impossible, for mind can only be produced by a previous moment of mind in its own continuum.

What connects one life with the next? Is there a soul, atman, self, or real personality that goes from one life to another?

Our mind has gross and subtle levels. The sense consciousnesses that see, hear, smell, taste and feel tactile sensations, and the gross mental consciousness, which is always so busy thinking this and that, function actively while we are alive. At the time of death, they cease to function and absorb into the subtle mental consciousness. This subtle mind bears with it the imprints of the actions we have done (karma). After death, the subtle mind leaves one body, enters the intermediate state and finally takes rebirth in another body. After the subtle mind joins with another body at the moment of conception, the gross sense consciousnesses and the gross mental consciousness reappear, and the person again sees, hears, thinks and so forth. This subtle mind, which goes from one life to the next, is a constantly changing phenomenon. For this reason, it is not considered to be a soul, atman, self or real personality. Thus the Buddha taught the doctrine of selflessness—that there is no solid, independent, findable thing that can be isolated as the person.

Do plants have mind? Are they sentient beings? Could a computer ever become a sentient being?

In general, plants are sentient beings. They are biologically alive, but that doesn't mean they have consciousness. Plants may react to music or to people talking to them, just as iron filings react to a magnet placed near them, but that doesn't indicate they have minds. However, in some rare cases, due to one's past actions, a person's mind may be attracted to a tree, for example, as its habitat.

When asked whether computers could have consciousness, His Holiness the Dalai Lama once responded that if at some point computers had the ability to act as a physical support for consciousness and if a person had created the karma to be reborn inside one, then a computer could become a sentient being!

How was the world created?

Anything that is created has arisen from causes that were able to produce it. Something can't be created out of nothing. The physical world of forms we see around us was produced by previous moments of form. This is the field investigated by scientists. They may find that our particular universe was created from subtler physical elements that, in turn, were a continuation from universes that existed before ours. In this way, we can trace the continuity of form back infinitely.

Is there one universal mind that we are all a part of?

According to Buddhism, no. Each of us has our own mindstream. However, when we purify our minds and become Buddhas, we will no longer have the feeling of being separate, isolated individuals. We will each be an individual Buddha, but we will have the same spiritual realizations. We won't feel cut off from each other.

Where did ignorance come from? Were we once enlightened and then became separated from that state?

No. Once someone is enlightened, there is no cause to again become confused or defiled. If the cause for imperfection exists in the mind, then the person is still ignorant. So, from a Buddhist viewpoint, we weren't once enlightened and then fell from that state because that would be impossible; there's no cause for that to happen. Although all sentient beings have the Buddha nature or Buddha potential, their minds have been clouded over by ignorance since beginningless time. Each moment of ignorance was produced from the preceding moment, without there being a beginning. No external being created it. However, although ignorance has no beginning, it does have an end. It can be removed through the wisdom realizing emptiness, the lack of fantasized ways of existing, because once we perceive reality, our minds can no longer ignorantly misconceive things.

What is the relationship between the brain and the mind?

The brain is a physical organ and is atomic in nature. The mind is formless and is characterized by clarity and awareness. While we're alive, our brain and mind influence each other. The brain provides the physical support for our sense consciousnesses and gross mental consciousness. If the brain and central nervous system are damaged, the functioning of the mind is affected. Similarly, our mental state—be it peaceful or agitated—affects our physical health and our nervous system.

There are subtler levels of mind that, according to Buddhism, don't rely on the physical body as a support. There is, for example, the subtlest mind, which continues on to the next life. Thus, skilled practitioners can meditate with their subtlest consciousness even after they are brain-dead. (The teacher who ordained me did this for thirteen days after the doctors pronounced him dead.) Scientists are very interested in studying this, and His Holiness the Dalai Lama has given his approval for scientists to measure great practitioners' brain functions at death and afterward. The problem is that it's difficult to schedule this so that the scientists are ready with their equipment in India when a great practitioner dies!

Why can't we remember our past lives?

At the moment, our minds are obscured by ignorance, making it difficult to remember the past. Also, many changes occur in our body and mind as we die and are reborn, making recollection difficult. However, the fact that we don't remember something, doesn't mean that it does not exist. Sometimes we can't even remember where we put our car keys! Nor can we remember what we ate for dinner a month ago!

Some people can remember their past lives. The Tibetans have a system of recognizing the reincarnations of highly realized masters. Quite often, as young children, these people will recognize their friends or possessions from a previous life. Some ordinary people too have had past life recall, sometimes in meditation or through hypnosis.

Is it important to know what our past lives were?

No. What's important is how we live our present life. Knowing what we were in past lives is useful only if it helps us to generate strong determination to avoid negative actions or to free ourselves from cyclic existence. To try to find out who we were in past lives only for curiosity's sake isn't useful. It could even lead us to become proud: "I was a king in my past life." "I was so famous and talented." "I was Einstein!" So what? Actually, we have all been and done everything in many past lives in cyclic existence. The important thing is to purify our previous negative actions, avoid creating more, and put energy into accumulating positive potential and developing our good qualities.

There's a Tibetan saying: "If you want to know about your past life, look at your present body. If you want to know your future life, look at your present mind." We received our present rebirth as a result of our past actions. A human rebirth is a fortunate one, and we created the cause for it by living ethically in our previous lives. On the other hand, our future rebirths will be determined by what we think, say and do now, and our mind motivates all these actions. Thus, we can get an idea of the kind of rebirths we will take by looking at our present attitudes and examining whether they are constructive or destructive. We don't need to go to a fortuneteller to ask what will become of us: we can simply consider the imprints we are leaving on our mindstream by our thoughts, words and deeds.

If everyone has had previous lives, how do you account for the population increase?

All the people alive now weren't necessarily human beings on planet Earth in their past lives. Their previous lives could have been as another life-form or in another universe. Earth is a tiny speck in the universe, and Buddhists believe that there is life in other places. Also, an animal, for example, could die and be reborn as a human.

Chapter 6

KARMA: THE FUNCTIONING OF CAUSE AND EFFECT

What is karma? How does it work?

Karma means action, and refers to intentional physical, verbal or mental actions. These actions leave imprints or seeds upon our mindstreams, and the imprints ripen into our experiences when the appropriate conditions come together. For example, with a kind heart we help someone. This action leaves an imprint on our mindstream, and when conditions are suitable, this imprint will ripen in our receiving help when we need it. The seeds of our actions continue with us from one lifetime to the next and do not get lost. However, if we don't create the cause or karma for something, then we won't experience that result: if a farmer doesn't plant seeds, nothing will grow. If an action brings about pain and misery in the long term, it is called negative, destructive or nonvirtuous. If it brings about happiness, it is called positive, constructive, or virtuous. Actions aren't inherently good or bad, but are only designated so according to the results they bring.

All results come from causes that have the ability to create them. If we plant apple seeds, an apple tree will grow, not chili. If chili seeds are planted, chili will grow, not apples. In the same way if we act constructively, happiness will ensue; if we act destructively, problems will result. Whatever happiness and fortune we experience in our lives comes from our own positive actions, while our problems result from our own destructive actions.

Is the law of actions and their effects a system of punishment and reward? Did the Buddha create or invent it?

Definitely not. According to Buddhism, there is no one in charge of the universe who distributes rewards and punishments. We create the causes by our actions, and we experience their results. We are responsible for our own experience. The Buddha didn't create the system of actions and their effects, in the same way that Newton didn't invent gravity. Newton simply described what exists. Likewise, the Buddha described what he saw with his omniscient mind to be the natural process of cause and effect occurring within the mindstream of each being. By doing this, he showed us how best to work within the functioning of cause and effect in order to experience happiness and avoid pain.

The misconception that happiness and pain are rewards and punishments may come from incorrect translations of Buddhist scriptures into English. I have seen some texts translated into English using terminology from other religions. This is very misleading because terms such as heaven, hell, sin, punishment, and judgment do not correspond to Buddhist concepts. Appropriate English words that convey the meaning of the Buddha's teachings must be used.

Does the law of actions and their effects apply only to people who believe in it?

No. Cause and effect functions whether we believe in it or not. Positive actions produce happiness and destructive ones result in pain whether we believe they will or not. If a fruit drops from a tree, it falls down even if we believe it will go up. It would be wonderful if all we needed to do to avoid the results of our actions was to believe they won't come! Then, for example, we could eat all we want and never get fat! People who don't believe in past lives and cause and effect can still experience happiness as a result of their actions in past lives. But by denying the existence of cause and effect, and consequently not attempting to practice constructive actions and avoid destructive ones, they may create few positive potentials and recklessly create many negative ones. On the other hand, people who know about cause and effect will try to be mindful of what they think, say and do to avoid hurting others and to avoid leaving harmful imprints on their own mindstreams.

What does karma affect?

Karma can affect our future rebirths, that is, the kind of life-form we will adopt. It also influences what we experience during our lives: how others treat us, our wealth, social status and so forth. Karma also affects our personality and character: our talents, dominant personality traits and habits. What kind of environment we're born into is also influenced by karma.

Why do some people who act destructively appear to be successful and happy? Why do some people who don't believe in the functioning of cause and effect have good lives?

When we see dishonest people who are wealthy, or cruel people who are powerful, or kind people who die young, we may doubt the law of actions and their effects. This is because we are looking only at the short period of this one life. Many of the results we experience in this life are the results of actions done in previous lives, and many of the actions we do in this life will ripen only in future lives. The wealth of dishonest people is the result of their generosity in preceding lives. Their current dishonesty is leaving the karmic seed for them to be cheated and to experience poverty in future lives. Likewise, the respect and authority given to cruel people is due to positive actions they did in the past. In the present, they are misusing their power, thus creating the cause for future pain. Kind people who die young are experiencing the result of negative actions such as killing done in past lives. However, their present kindness is planting seeds or imprints on their mindstreams for them to experience happiness in the future.

The scriptures spoken by the Buddha outline general guidelines about the results of various actions. However, only a Buddha's omniscient mind can understand completely specific details of the ripening of karma. For example, the scriptures tell us that killing causes a short life and generosity results in wealth. But we ordinary beings aren't capable of knowing for certain who our friend Susan was in a past life, whom she was generous toward and what she gave that resulted in her being rich in this life.

There is flexibility in the functioning of actions and their results. While we know that insulting others, for example, brings us an unfortunate rebirth, just exactly what body we're born into can vary. If the action was very heavy—for example, with strong anger we repeatedly abused many people and afterward felt gratified that we had hurt their feelings—the result will be more unpleasant than if we casually teased someone once and later regretted our insensitivity. The conditions present at the time that karmic seed ripens will also influence what specific result it brings.

Do we create karma together as a group?

Yes. Karma is both collective and individual. Collective karma are the actions we do together as a group: soldiers use weapons, a group of religious practitioners pray or meditate. The results of these actions are experienced together as a group, often in future lives. Yet each member of a group thinks, speaks and acts slightly differently, thus creating individual karma, the results of which each person will experience him- or herself.

Do we necessarily experience the results of all of our actions?

When seeds, even small ones, are planted in the ground, they will eventually sprout—that is, unless they don't receive the necessary conditions for growth such as water, sunshine and fertilizer, or they are burnt or pulled out of the ground. The ultimate way to uproot karmic imprints or seeds is by meditation on the emptiness of inherent existence. This is the way to purify the disturbing attitudes and the karmic imprints completely. At our level, this may be rather difficult, but we can still stop the harmful imprints from ripening by purifying them. This is similar to preventing the seed from receiving water, sunshine and fertilizer.

How can we purify negative imprints?

Purification by means of the four opponent powers is very important. It not only prevents future suffering, but also relieves guilt. By cleansing our minds, we'll be able to concentrate and to understand the Dharma better, and we'll be more peaceful. The four opponent powers used to purify negative imprints or seeds are:
1. regret,
2. determination not to do the action again,
3. taking refuge and generating an altruistic attitude toward others, and
4. an actual remedial practice.

First, we acknowledge and regret that we have acted destructively. This is different from having self-recrimination and guilt, which are useless and keep us bound up in anxiety. With sincere regret, on the other hand, we simply acknowledge that we made a mistake and regret doing it.

Secondly, we make a determination not to do the action again. If the action is habitual and frequent—for example, criticizing others—it would be hypocritical to say we will never do it again the rest of our lives. It's better to determine that we will try not to repeat the action again, but will be especially mindful and make a concerted effort during a realistic, set period of time, such as a few days.

The third opponent power is to take refuge and generate altruism. Our destructive actions are generally in relation to either holy objects such as the Buddhas, Dharma and Sangha, or other sentient beings. To reestablish a good relationship with the holy objects, we seek their guidance by taking refuge in them. To restore our good relationships with other sentient beings, we generate an altruistic attitude toward them by aspiring to become a Buddha so we can best benefit them.

The fourth opponent power is to do a remedial action. This may be any positive action: listening to teachings, reading a Dharma book, bowing to the Three Jewels, making offerings, reciting the names of the Buddhas, chanting mantras, making statues or paintings of the Buddhas, printing texts, meditating and so on. We can also offer service in the community, aiding those in difficulty, or offer service to a Dharma center or temple. The most powerful remedial action is to meditate on emptiness, as nonconceptual wisdom directly uproots the negative imprints so that they can never bear fruit.

The four opponent powers must be done repeatedly. We have done negative actions many times, so naturally we can't expect to counteract all of them at once. The stronger the four opponents powers are—the stronger our regret, the firmer our determination not to do the action again, and so on—the more powerful the purification will be. It's especially effective to purify using the four opponent powers every evening before going to sleep to counteract any destructive actions we have done during the day.

If people suffer because of their own negative actions, does that mean that we cannot or should not do anything to help them?

Not at all! We know what it's like to feel miserable, and that is exactly how others feel when they are experiencing the results of their own destructive actions. Out of empathy and compassion, we should definitely help! Their present predicament was brought about by their own actions, but that doesn't mean that we should stand by and say, "Oh that's too bad. You poor thing. You shouldn't have done such destructive actions."

Karma isn't inflexible or cast in concrete. It doesn't mean fate or predetermination. Yes, people created the cause to experience difficulties, but maybe they also created the cause to receive help from us! We are all alike in wanting happiness and trying to avoid pain. It doesn't matter whose pain or problem it is, we can try to relieve it. For example, to think, "The poor are poor because of their own past lives' miserliness. I would be interfering with their karma if I tried to help," is a cruel misconception. We shouldn't try to rationalize our own laziness, apathy or smugness by misinterpreting cause and effect. Compassion and universal responsibility are important for our own spiritual development and for world peace. They are the cornerstones of all Buddhist practice.

Does karma influence whom we will meet and the relationships we'll have with them?

Yes, but this doesn't mean that relationships are predetermined. We may have certain karmic predispositions to feel close to or to have friction with certain people. But, this doesn't mean that our relationships with them must continue along the same lines. If we're kind to those who speak ill of us and try to communicate with them, the relationships will change. We'll also create positive karma, which will bring happiness in the future.

We aren't karmically bound to others. Nor are there "soul mates," special people who are the one and only one for us. Since we've had infinite past lives, we've had contact with every being sometime before. Also, our relationship with any particular person constantly changes. Nonetheless, past karmic connections can influence our present relationships. For example, if someone has been our spiritual mentor in a past life, we may be drawn to that person in this lifetime, and when he or she teaches us the Dharma, it may have a very strong effect on our minds.

Can people be reborn as animals and animals as people? How is that karmically possible?

Yes. Based on our actions, our minds are attracted toward certain types of rebirth when we die. It may seem difficult to imagine that a human being could be reborn as an animal, but if we consider the fact that some people act worse than animals, it doesn't seem so farfetched. For example, animals kill only when they are threatened or hungry, while some human beings kill for sport, fame or power. If someone's mind habitually goes in a certain direction, it makes sense that his or her body could correspond to that mental state in a future life.

Similarly, animals can be reborn as humans. Although it's difficult for most animals to do many positive actions (it's hard to teach a dog to meditate or to offer community service), it is possible. That's why the Tibetans take their animals when they circumambulate holy monuments: it puts good imprints on the animals' minds. Also, humans can have both positive and negative karmic imprints on their minds. If someone is angry at the time he dies, some of the negative imprints could ripen and he could be reborn as a dog. However, the positive imprints still remain on his mindstream and when causes and conditions come together, they could ripen, causing him to again be born as a human.

Chapter 7

DYING, DEATH AND
THE INTERMEDIATE STATE

How can we best help someone who is dying or dead?
When people are terminally ill, we can help them arrange all their worldly affairs while their bodies and minds are still strong. In this way, they can put to rest their worries and concerns about money and family. It's helpful if they can give away their belongings because they create much good karma through generosity and this will help them in future lives. Generosity also frees them from attachment, which is very harmful at the time of death. We can also encourage people to resolve any grudges or remorse they may have, either by discussing their feelings with the other people concerned or by doing purification practices. By thus freeing their minds from anger and guilt, they can die peacefully.

If it's not possible to help people prepare for death in this way, then as death approaches, we can assure them that their worldly affairs will be taken care of after they pass away. They needn't be concerned about who will pay the bills or take care of the children. They should concentrate on leaving this life peacefully, without fears or worries. Don't bother people by asking, "Who will get your jewelry?" or "Do you have any hidden money?" or "How will I live without you?" Our motivation is to help dying people, not to give them more problems!

When people are dying, it's best to create an environment that is calm and free from people and things that could evoke their attachment or anger. It's difficult to die peacefully if the entire family is in the room crying, grasping the person's hand, and pleading, "Please don't die. We love you. How can you leave us alone?" We may think we are expressing our love and concern by acting this way, but actually, it's our selfish mind wailing because we're losing someone we care about. We should try to care more about the dying person's needs than our own and make the environment calm and pleasant.

During a person's final hours before death, it is recommended to discontinue all invasive treatment—monitors, IVs and so on. This allows the person to turn his or her thoughts inward and prepare to die without being distracted by external commotion. It also permits the physical energies to dissolve in a more natural way.

It's harmful if people die with anger or attachment, jealousy or pride as their last thought. Thus, we should try to create a quiet and calm environment and encourage them to generate positive thoughts. If they are Buddhist, we can talk about the Buddha, Dharma and Sangha and remind them of their spiritual masters. We can show them pictures of the Buddha or chant some prayers and mantras in the room. Before death actually occurs, try to guide them to purify their destructive actions. Encourage them to pray for a good rebirth, to meet pure teachings and teachers and to make their death, intermediate state and rebirth life beneficial for others.

If people are of other faiths, it's unwise to push our faith on them at the time of death. That could cause confusion in their minds. It's best to speak according to their faith and to encourage them to generate positive states of mind.

Are people reborn immediately after death or is there an intermediate state before the next rebirth?

The heart and breath may stop and people may be brain-dead, but their subtlest consciousness may still remain connected to the body for up to three days. Highly realized masters may even meditate for weeks after their vital signs have ceased, before their subtlest consciousness leaves their body. For that reason, it's recommended to leave the body undisturbed for several days or at least for a few hours if possible. Then, it's advised to touch the crown of the person's head, because if the consciousness can leave from that point, it's auspicious for the next life.

After an ordinary person's mind leaves the gross physical body, it enters an intermediate stage (*bardo* in Tibetan) before it assumes another gross body. Depending on conditions, a person may remain in the intermediate stage for only a few moments, or for as long as forty-nine days. Although I've asked several teachers, I haven't discovered why it's forty-nine days, rather than another number. In certain cases, the person is reborn immediately, without staying in the intermediate state.

Beings in the intermediate state have subtle bodies that aren't made of atoms and are similar to the bodies they will take in their next rebirth. For a while they may try to communicate with their friends or relatives from their previous life, but intermediate state beings aren't able to communicate with human beings. After forty-nine days they have definitely taken new bodies and are absorbed in the experiences of their new lives.

Can someone be reborn as a spirit? How do we account for channeling or for people who talk to a dead relative through a medium?

Some people have created the causes to be reborn as spirits. Spirits belong to a realm of life-forms called hungry ghosts, which is considered an unfortunate rebirth. Spirits and sometimes gods can channel through mediums, but all these beings are still bound to cyclic existence by their ignorance, attachment and anger. Some may have clairvoyant powers, some may not; some may tell the truth, some may not. Spiritual channeling isn't always reliable. There's no need to try to contact dead friends and relatives. It's more worthwhile to communicate well with them and be kind to them now, while they're alive.

Does chanting for the dead help? What else can be done for them?

After death, chanting the sutras and doing other Buddhist practices can be helpful by stimulating the deceased's own positive potential to ripen. Although they have already left their physical body and can't hear the chanting with their ears, our creating positive potential and dedicating it for their welfare can help. It's helpful to do such virtuous practices each week for seven weeks after their death. This is because if they haven't already found another gross body to take rebirth in, they remain in the intermediate stage. The positive potential we create and dedicate for them can help them find a good rebirth. However, don't think, "I'll ask some monks and nuns to do the chanting while I go about my business." We have a karmic relationship with the deceased, so the prayers and virtuous activities that we dedicate for their benefit are important too.

It's helpful to offer the deceased's possessions to others as a way of practicing generosity and accumulating positive potential. Offering to holy objects (Buddha, Dharma, Sangha) and to the poor and sick is especially beneficial. We can then dedicate the positive potential from this for the benefit of all sentient beings and especially for the deceased.

Some Asians leave out food for the deceased and burn paper money and houses for the deceased. Is this necessary or beneficial?

It's said that intermediate state beings survive by "eating" smells, so leaving out food may be helpful during the forty-nine days after death. After that the deceased have been reborn in a happy or unfortunate rebirth according to their previous actions. After they have been born, the food set out never reaches them. Most likely there is food available wherever they have been reborn. However, we can offer food to beings born as hungry ghosts—be they our former relatives and friends or not—by reciting certain mantras over extra food. These mantras help to eliminate the hungry ghosts' karmic obscurations to finding food.

Burning paper cars, clothes or money doesn't give the deceased these things in their future rebirth. It's not necessary to burn all these things. The tradition of doing so is an old Chinese custom, not a practice taught by the Buddha. If we want to help our relatives and friends to have wealth in their future lives, we should encourage them to make offerings and be generous while they are alive. The Buddha said generosity is the cause of wealth, not burning papers.

Sometimes, we may advise our relatives, "Don't give away so much. Our family won't have so much money if you do." By encouraging them to be miserly, we cause them to plant the seeds on their mindstreams to be poor in their future lives. Also, we plant the same kind of seed on our own mindstreams. On the other hand, encouraging them to be generous and to avoid cheating others in business helps them to be wealthy in the future.

If we want our loved ones to have a good rebirth, the best help we can give is to encourage them while they are alive to avoid the ten destructive actions and to practice the ten constructive ones which are their opposites. The ten destructive actions are killing, stealing, unwise sexual behavior, lying, slander, harsh speech, gossip, coveting others' possessions, maliciousness and wrong views. If we encourage them to lie to protect us or to cheat someone so we can have more, we're helping them to create the cause for unfortunate rebirths. Should we spend hours gossiping with them, drinking and criticizing others, we're defeating our own purpose. Since we sincerely want them to be happy after death, we should help them abandon these destructive actions and practice constructive ones. We can encourage (but not force) them to take ethical precepts. That is really acting to benefit their future lives.

What is the Buddhist view on suicide?

It is considered a great tragedy. Human life is precious and it's a tragedy when people become so overwhelmed by their disturbing attitudes that they see death as the only way to stop their suffering. In fact, suicide doesn't really solve the problem because they will be reborn. Also, people who kill themselves are generally experiencing much anger, jealousy or other disturbing attitudes at the time of death, and this could adversely affect their future rebirth.

Buddhists believe that all beings have the Buddha potential or Buddha nature, the potential to become fully enlightened. The disturbing attitudes are like clouds obscuring the pure nature of our minds, but they aren't part of us. They are fleeting, and through Dharma practice, we can remove them entirely. If people could get even an inkling of this, they wouldn't take their own misery so seriously and would be confident in their own inner goodness. This new perspective may help them decide to continue living because they recognize a reliable way to stop their problems.

What is the Buddhist view on euthanasia?

From the Buddhist viewpoint, it's generally considered better to preserve life. However, each situation is different and must be looked at individually. In many cases, there are no easy answers. If we know that a person who is comatose or who is in great pain will be reborn in a happier situation, then motivated by compassion, we could consider mercy killing. However, as most of us lack such clairvoyance, it's extremely difficult to know whether we would be helping or harming another by mercy killing. It's possible that the seed of a previous negative action will ripen and that person will be reborn in a situation which is worse than the present one. It also happens that people come out of coma and live for many years.

If people understand the value of human life—how precious it is for practicing the path to enlightenment—they may be able to transform painful situations into the path. For example, people may be bedridden, but if their minds are alert, they can practice the Dharma, increase their good qualities, purify their negative actions and practice the path to enlightenment. In fact, they may have more time to do this than people who are so busy running here and there! There are Buddhist practices especially designed for transforming adverse conditions into the path, and we could learn those and teach them to those who are very ill. Also, I have spoken to people who have been in comas, and several of them said that they were aware of their environment. Thus, reading prayers or reciting mantras near comatose people could help them. Even if their minds are obscured, hearing the Dharma leaves beneficial imprints on their minds.

When people make "living wills" stating their preferences for medical treatment if they are severely injured or ill, it reduces their families' anxiety should such unfortunate events occur. It is not an act of killing not to put someone on a life support system when there is no hope for his or her recovery. This is simply letting nature take its course, and may allow the person to die more peacefully than if invasive or forceful measures were employed. However, once someone is on a life-support system, the issue becomes more complicated. Each situation needs to be considered separately because many factors are involved: the dying person's own wishes, the severity of his or her condition, the person's level of conscious awareness, his or her spiritual preparedness for death and emotional state, and the emotional and financial toll on the family. There is no one answer suitable for all cases. We must act with as much compassion and wisdom as we can when faced with such difficult decisions.

Because funding for medical research and health care is limited, our society could allocate most of those funds to improve prenatal care and education, thus improving the quality of life. In this way, people wouldn't be faced with so many ethical and emotional dilemmas near the time of death.

Chapter 8

THE BUDDHIST TRADITIONS

What are the Buddhist scriptures called?

The scriptures spoken by the Buddha fall into two general categories: the sutras and the tantras. The sutras deal with the trainings in ethics, concentration and wisdom as well as the development of altruism and the general practices undertaken with that motivation. The tantras describe practices unique to Vajrayana. The Buddha spoke both the sutras and tantras during his lifetime. His direct disciples memorized them and later generations recorded them in writing.

Why are there many Buddhist traditions?

The Buddha gave a wide variety of teachings because sentient beings (beings with mind who are not yet Buddhas) have different dispositions, inclinations and interests. The Buddha never expected us all to fit the same mold. Thus, with skill and compassion in guiding others, he offered several philosophical systems and ways of practicing so that each of us could find something that suits our inclinations and personality. The essence of all his teachings is the same: the determination to be free from cyclic existence; love, compassion and altruism toward others; and the wisdom realizing reality.

Not everyone likes the same kind of food. At a huge buffet dinner, we can choose the dishes we like. We don't need to like everything. Although we may have a taste for sweets, that doesn't mean that the salty dishes aren't good and should be thrown away! Similarly, we may prefer a certain approach to the teachings: Theravada, Pure Land, Zen, Vajrayana, and so on. We are free to choose the approach that suits us best and with which we feel the most comfortable. However, it's important to maintain an open mind and respect for other traditions. As our minds develop, we may come to understand elements in other traditions that we failed to comprehend previously. In short, we should practice whatever we find useful to help us live a better life, and we can leave aside without criticizing whatever we do not yet understand.

Although we may find one particular tradition best suited for our personality, it's not wise to identify with it too strongly: "*I* am a Mahayanist, *you* are a Theravadin," or "*I* am a Buddhist, *you* are a Christian." It is important to re-member that we are all human beings who seek happiness and want to realize the truth, and we each must find a method that suits our disposition.

However, keeping an open mind to different approaches doesn't mean mixing everything together at random, making our practice like chop suey. Avoid mixing meditation tech-niques from different traditions together in one meditation session. In one session, it is better to do one technique. If we take a little of this technique and a little from that, and with-out understanding either one very well mix them together, we may end up confused. However, a teaching emphasized in one tradition may enrich our understanding and practice of another. Also, it is advisable to do the same meditations daily. If we do breathing meditation one day, chanting the Buddha's name the next, and analytical meditation the third, we won't make progress in any of them for there is no contitinuity in the practice. However, we can do all three each day, thus maintaining continuity in our practice.

What are the various Buddhist traditions?

Generally, there are two divisions: Theravada and Mahayana. The Theravada lineage (Tradition of the Elders), which relies on sutras recorded in the Pali language, spread from India to Sri Lanka, Thailand, Burma, etc. It emphasizes meditation on the breath to develop concentration and meditation on mindfulness of the body, feelings, mind and phenomena in order to develop wisdom. In Pali, these two types of meditation are called samatha and vipassana.

The Mahayana (Great Vehicle) tradition, based on the scriptures recorded in Sanskrit, spread to China, Tibet, Japan, Korea, Vietnam, etc. Although love and compassion are essential and important factors in Theravada Buddhism, they are emphasized to an even greater extent in Mahayana Buddhism. Within Mahayana, there are several branches: Pure Land emphasizes chanting the name of Amitabha Buddha in order to be reborn in his pure land, a place where all conditions are conducive to Dharma practice; Zen emphasizes meditation to eliminate the noisy, conceptual mind; Vajrayana (Diamond Vehicle) employs meditation on a deity in order to transform our contaminated body and mind into those of a Buddha.

The fact that there is a variety of practices within the Buddhist doctrine attests to the Buddha's skill in being able to guide people according to their dispositions and needs. It is extremely important not to be partial and sectarian, but to have respect for all the traditions and their practitioners.

Why do some monks and nuns wear saffron robes while others are dressed in maroon, gray or black?

As the Buddha's teaching spread from one country to another, it adapted to the culture and mentality of the people in each place without changing its essential meaning. Thus, the style of the Sangha's robes varies. In Sri Lanka, Thailand, Burma, Cambodia, etc., the robes are saffron-colored and sleeveless, the way the robes were at the time of the Buddha. People who have taken the eight precepts and aren't technically monks or nuns wear white robes.

Saffron dye wasn't available in Tibet, so a deeper color, maroon, was used. In China it was considered impolite to expose the skin, so the long-sleeved costume of the T'ang Dynasty was adopted. Also, the Chinese considered saffron too bright for those on a religious path, and changed the color of the robes to gray. However, the spirit of the original robes was kept in the form of the seven- and nine-piece brown, yellow and red outer robes that the monks and nuns wear while praying.

Chanting styles vary in the various Buddhist countries, corresponding to the culture and language of the place. The musical instruments and the way of bowing differ as well. For example, the Chinese stand up while chanting while the Tibetans sit down. These variations are due to cultural adaptations. It's important to understand that these external forms and ways of doing things are not the Dharma. They are tools to help us practice the Dharma better according to the culture and place in which we live. The real Dharma can't be seen with our eyes or heard with our ears. It is to be experienced by our minds and hearts. We must direct our attention to the real Dharma, not to the superficial appearances that may vary from place to place.

Chapter 9

VAJRAYANA

What is Vajrayana? What are the special qualities of Vajrayana practice?

Vajrayana, also called Tantrayana, is a subdivision of the Mahayana. It's based upon general Mahayana practices. Vajrayana is widespread in Tibet and is practiced by the Japanese Shingon tradition as well.

One technique used in Vajrayana is visualizing oneself as a deity and the environment as the mandala or the environment of the deity. Using imagination in this way, Vajrayana practitioners transform their ordinary poor self-image into that of fully enlightened Buddhas, and thus try to cultivate the noble qualities of the Buddhas in their own mind-streams. In other words, rather than get locked into ordinary feelings of low self-esteem and lack of confidence, they imagine what it would feel like to be impartially compassionate toward all beings and to perceive the empty nature of all phenomena. Doing this functions psychologically to give them the energy and ability to progress along the path and actually develop those qualities.

Vajrayana contains techniques for transforming death, the intermediate state and rebirth into the body and mind of a Buddha. It also has special meditative techniques to develop calm abiding (samatha) as well as to make manifest an extremely subtle mind, which, when realizing emptiness, becomes very powerful in quickly cleansing defilements from the mind. For this reason Vajrayana can bring enlightenment in this very lifetime if one is a qualified and well-trained student who practices under the guidance of a fully qualified tantric master.

Buddhist Tantra is not the same as Hindu Tantra, nor is it the practice of magic. Some people have written books about Vajrayana with incorrect information and interpretations. Therefore, if we wish to learn about this practice, it's important to either read books by knowledgeable authors or seek instruction from qualified masters.

What is an empowerment? Why are some teachings "secret"?

The purpose of empowerment is to ripen one's mind-stream for the tantric practice by making a connection with the deity, who is a manifestation of the omniscient minds. One can't receive empowerment merely by being present in the room where an empowerment is taking place. Rather, people must meditate and visualize as the master instructs. Nor is empowerment having a vase placed on one's head, or drinking blessed water, or tying a consecrated string around one's arm. An empowerment ripens one's own potential through making a connection with a particular manifestation of the Buddha. This depends on having a virtuous motivation and on concentrating and meditating during the empowerment ceremony.

After empowerment, sincere practitioners seek instructions on how to do the practice. These instructions are not given before the empowerment because the students' minds aren't yet prepared to practice them. For this reason they are "secret." It's not that the Buddha was miserly and didn't want to share the teachings, nor is tantric practice the possession of an exclusive club that jealously guards its secrets. Rather, tantric instruction is given only to those who have received empowerment to ensure that those engaging in the practice have been properly prepared. Otherwise, someone might misunderstand the symbolism employed in the tantra or engage in advanced and complex practices without proper preparation and instruction.

At what point does someone take a tantric empowerment?

Before entering the Vajrayana, one must be well-trained in the determination to be free from cyclic existence, the altruistic intention and the wisdom realizing the emptiness of inherent existence. One then takes an empowerment (initiation) from a qualified tantric master and follows the tantric vows and commitments taken at the time of empowerment. On this basis, one receives instructions and practices the Vajrayana meditations. Initiations are not ends in themselves: they are a gateway into further practice. So sincere students take empowerments because they want to practice the teachings afterward.

Why are empowerments given so openly to newcomers if people need a firm foundation in general Buddhist practices to practice Tantra effectively?

Many lamas (Tibetan spiritual masters) believe that although people may not be fully prepared to do the Vajrayana practice, positive imprints are put on their mindstreams by taking empowerments and thus making a karmic connection to the practice.

However, since taking tantric empowerments often involves taking vows and commitments and promising to do a certain meditation practice daily, it's wise for people to consider carefully before rushing into high practices. When Dharma centers announce an empowerment, they should also tell people which vows and commitments are involved and which practices must be done afterward. Also, people should examine the qualities of a spiritual master to make that sure he or she is qualified and that they want to form a teacher-student relationship with that person. It's wise to go slowly, developing one's Dharma practice gradually, rather than jumping into high practices thinking "this is the one and only opportunity." Also, one needn't run around taking every empowerment that is offered. It's better to take fewer empowerments but to practice them well, than to run around proudly collecting empowerments but practicing very little.

What does the imagery in tantric art mean?

Vajrayana deals with transformation, and therefore symbolism is widely used. All the tantric deities are manifestations of fully enlightened, compassionate Buddhas, yet the appearance of some of these deities is ferocious or desirous. The sexual imagery isn't to be taken literally, according to worldly appearances. In Vajrayana, the depiction of deities in sexual union represents the union of method and wisdom, the two aspects of the path that must be developed to attain enlightenment. Ferocious looking deities aren't monsters who threaten us. Their wrath is directed toward ignorance and selfishness, which are our real enemies. This imagery, when properly understood, shows how desire and anger can be transformed and thereby subdued. It has deep meaning, far beyond ordinary lust and anger. One should avoid misinterpreting it.

Who are the Dharma protectors?

These are beings who have promised to help safeguard the existence of the Dharma in our world and to protect the people who practice it. They are generally fierce in appearance, but their wrath is directed toward the ignorance producing the misunderstandings, disharmony, and degeneration that destroy the Dharma. Some Dharma protectors are transworldly, that is, they are manifestations of Buddhas, or bodhisattvas who have direct perception of emptiness. Others are beings within cyclic existence who have promised the Buddhas that they would protect the Dharma. Dharma protectors are found in most Buddhist traditions, not just the Vajrayana.

Vajrayana seems to be full of colorful and elaborate rituals. Where is the meditation?

Public Vajrayana ceremonies may appear very ritualistic, but the rituals aren't ends in themselves. They are guided meditations in which the practitioners try to generate the meanings of the prayers in their minds. When these same practices are done privately, practitioners can shorten the recitations and pause for long periods to practice concentration and insight meditation, or to meditate on loving-kindness.

Chapter 10

STEPS ALONG THE PATH

What is an arhat (*arahat*)? What is nirvana (*nibbana*)?

An arhat is someone who has eliminated the ignorance and disturbing attitudes (anger, attachment, jealousy, pride, etc.) from his or her mind forever. In addition, he or she has purified all karma that could cause rebirth in cyclic existence (samsara). An arhat abides in a state of peace, which is called nirvana or liberation and is beyond all unsatisfactory experiences and confusion.

What is bodhi or enlightenment?

In addition to eliminating ignorance, disturbing attitudes and contaminated actions (*karma*) from their minds, Buddhas have also eliminated the stains of these defilements and have fully developed the altruistic intention that cherishes others more than self. Thus Buddhas have attained full enlightenment, the state in which all defilements have been purified and all good qualities developed.

What is a bodhisattva?

A bodhisattva is someone who spontaneously and continuously has the wish to attain enlightenment for the benefit of sentient beings. By practicing the path, such a person will attain the state of Buddhahood.

There are different levels of bodhisattvas, according to their level of realization. Some are not yet free from cyclic existence, while others are. The latter can then voluntarily continue to take birth in the world by the power of their compassion to help others. Buddhas can do this as well.

Do bodhisattvas give up attaining enlightenment and stay in this world to help others?

Some scriptures say that bodhisattvas vow to stay in cyclic existence and not attain enlightenment until all beings have been liberated from cyclic existence. This means that bodhisattvas' compassion for sentient beings is so strong that if it were beneficial, they would happily sacrifice their own liberation for that of others. However, bodhisattvas are also practical and realize that to help others most effectively, they need to become Buddhas themselves because only Buddhas have the full compassion, wisdom and skill needed to best benefit others. Thus bodhisattvas seek to attain full enlightenment, but when they do they don't remain in their own blissful state and forget about others. They manifest in forms that can skillfully guide others.

What is an arya, a superior or noble one?

This is a person who has direct realization of emptiness. Such a realization occurs before one becomes an arhat or Buddha, and with this wisdom realizing emptiness one eliminates ignorance, disturbing attitudes, contaminated karma, and their stains, thereby attaining liberation and enlightenment.

Chapter 11

EMOTIONS

**What role do emotions play in Buddhist practice?
Does the Buddha have emotions?**

Some emotions are realistic and constructive, others aren't.
Thus, some are to be cultivated on the path and others
abandoned. The Buddha taught various antidotes to counteract negative emotions such as anger, attachment, jealousy
and pride. He also taught techniques to cultivate genuine
love and compassion. According to Buddhism, love is the
wish for all others to have happiness and its causes, and
compassion is the wish for them to be free of difficulties and
their causes. Such love and compassion are extended equally
to all beings, and the Buddha taught a step-by-step method
for developing them. Buddhas have positive emotions such
as these.

**What is the difference between being attached to
other people and loving them? Why is attachment
problematic?**

In Buddhism, attachment is defined as an attitude that exaggerates other people's good qualities or projects good
qualities that aren't there and then clings to these people.
With attachment, we care for others because they please us:
they give us presents, praise us, help and encourage us. On
the other hand, love is wanting others to be happy simply

74

because they are living beings just like ourselves. When we are attached to others, we don't see them for who they are and thereby develop many expectations of them: they should be like this, they should do that. Then, when they don't live up to what we thought they were or should be, we feel hurt, disillusioned or angry. Love doesn't expect anything from others in return. We accept people for who they are and try to help them, but we aren't concerned with how we'll benefit from the relationship. Real love isn't jealous, possessive or limited to just a few near and dear ones. Rather, it's impartial and is felt for all beings.

If we're detached, is it possible to be with our friends and family?

"Detachment" isn't an accurate translation of the Buddhist concept; "nonattachment" may be better. Detachment implies being uninvolved, cold and aloof. However, in the Buddhist sense, it means having a balanced attitude, free from clinging. When we are free from attachment, we won't have unrealistic expectations of others, nor will we cling to them out of fear of being miserable when they aren't around. Nonattachment is a calm, realistic, open and accepting attitude. It isn't hostile, paranoid or unsociable. Having a balanced attitude doesn't mean rejecting our friends and family: it means relating to them in a different way. When we aren't attached, our relationships with others are harmonious, and in fact, our affection for them increases.

Are all desires bad? What about the desire to attain nirvana or enlightenment?

This confusion occurs because sometimes the English word "desire" is used to translate two different Buddhist concepts. There are different kinds of desire. The desire that is problematic exaggerates the good qualities of an object, person or idea and clings to it. Such desire is a form of attachment. An example is being very emotionally dependent on someone and clinging to him or her. When we look with a more balanced attitude, we'll see that the other person isn't nearly as fantastic as our attachment leads us to believe.

On the other hand, the desire that spurs us to prepare for future lives or to attain nirvana or enlightenment is completely different. Here we realize that better states of being are possible and we develop a realistic aspiration to achieve them. No misconceptions are involved, nor is there clinging to the desired result.

Wouldn't life be boring without attachment?

No. In fact it's attachment that makes us restless and prevents us from enjoying things. For example, suppose we're attached to chocolate cake. Even while we're eating it, we're not tasting it and enjoying it completely. We're usually either criticizing ourselves for eating something fattening, comparing the taste of this chocolate cake to other cakes we've eaten in the past, or planning how to get another piece. In any case, we're not really experiencing the chocolate cake in the present.

On the other hand, without attachment, we can think clearly about whether we want to eat the cake, and if we decide to, we can eat it peacefully, tasting and enjoying every bite without craving for more or being dissatisfied because it isn't as good as we expected.

As we diminish our attachment, life becomes more interesting because we're able to open up to what's happening in each moment. For example, rather than wishing we were with the people to whom we're attached, we'll appreciate being with whomever we're spending time with at present. Instead of being attached to our physical appearance and consequently feeling constant dissatisfaction with how we look, we'll simply do what's needed to be well groomed and will be satisfied with how we look.

How can we pursue our career without attachment to reputation and wealth? How can we do business and also be ethical?

If we deeply contemplate the transient and unpredictable nature of wealth, reputation, and worldly success, the belief that they'll bring us lasting happiness will fade. Then we can start to change our motivation for working. We can look at our work as service to society and as an opportunity to learn more about ourselves by interacting with others. Our work will thus become an occasion to practice the teachings that we meditate on. Then patience and cherishing others won't remain traits we cultivate only in meditation, but qualities we live by in daily life.

If we diminish our attachment, we'll find it easier to live ethically. As our priorities change, we'll be fair in our business dealings and won't backbite to climb the corporate ladder. Although some people think it's necessary to be unethical to succeed in business, one successful business executive told me that the opposite is the case. When we deal fairly with clients, they trust us, continue to do business with us and bring in new customers. When we treat our colleagues respectfully, they generally reciprocate, and we avoid becoming entangled in office politics. Should others mistreat us, we can work on practicing tolerance and developing better communication skills. Our feeling of being successful human beings won't depend on money and fame. We'll feel better about ourselves and have less guilt because we'll be living ethically. That will actually save money, because we don't need to go to a psychiatrist!

How can we deal with fear?

Fear is closely related to attachment. The more attached we are to someone or something, the more we fear not getting it or being separated from it. For example, if we're very attached to and emotionally dependent on a particular person, then we fear the relationship will end. If we're attached to money and financial security, then we are anxious about not having enough. If we're attached to our image, then we fear looking stupid in front of others.

On one hand, it's normal to have such concerns because we've been raised to be attached to these things. On the other hand, clinging makes us fearful and anxious. The solution isn't to abandon our friends, money and reputation but to let go of the attachment to them. Then we can enjoy them free from fear.

Can one be attached to Buddhism? What should we do if someone attacks our beliefs and criticizes the Dharma?

Each situation must be regarded individually. In general, if we feel "They are criticizing my beliefs. They think I am stupid for believing that," then we're clinging to our beliefs. We're thinking, "These beliefs are good because they are *mine*. If someone criticizes them, they are criticizing *me*." Such an attitude isn't very productive and we'll be more peaceful if we abandon it. We are not our beliefs. If others disagree with our beliefs, it doesn't mean we're stupid. It's helpful to be open to what others say. Let's not be attached to the name and label of our religion. We are seeking truth and happiness, not promotion of a religion because it happens to be ours. The Buddha himself said we should check his teachings and not just believe in them blindly.

On the other hand, this doesn't mean that we should automatically agree with everything someone else says. We shouldn't abandon our beliefs and adopt theirs indiscriminately. If someone asks a question we can't answer, it doesn't mean the Buddha's teachings are wrong. It simply means we don't know the answer and need to learn and contemplate more. We can then take the question to knowledgeable Buddhists and think about their answers. When others question our beliefs, they are actually helping us deepen our understanding of the Buddha's teachings by showing us what we don't yet understand. This inspires us to study the Dharma and reflect on its meaning more deeply.

We needn't defend our beliefs to someone else. If people ask questions with sincere interest and are open-minded and interested in a real exchange of views, then talking with them can be mutually enriching. However, if people really don't want a response and just want to antagonize or confuse us, then dialogue is impossible. There is no need to feel defensive in front of such people—we don't have to prove anything to them. Even if we were to give them logical answers, they aren't really listening because they're involved with their own preconceptions. Without being rude, we can be quite firm and end the conversation.

What can we do about stress?

Stress can be caused by a number of factors, some external and some internal. When we're stressed because there's not enough time and we feel pressured, it's helpful to think about our priorities and decide what things are most important in our lives. Then we can choose to do those things and put the others on the back burner. When we're stressed because we don't have the ability to do something that's expected of us, we need to accept our limitations. We aren't failures because we lack certain abilities. We need to communicate honestly with the people who hold such expectations of us. When we're stressed due to illness or sudden changes in our living situation, it's helpful to reflect on impermanence—that everything in our world will change. Then we can adapt to the change rather than fight it.

Much of our stress is due to not accepting the reality of a situation. We want it to be different or we want ourselves or others to be different. However, what is happening at the moment is what exists. Instead of rejecting the situation, which causes us more anxiety, we can accept it and work with it. Accepting whatever is happening isn't being fatalistic; it's being realistic. Having accepted the reality of the situation for what it presently is, we can still try to improve it in the future, while remaining realistic about what is possible.

Calming the mind through breathing meditation counteracts stress. So does meditating on patience and compassion. Purification meditation is helpful as well. For this reason, daily meditation is recommended to prevent and counteract stress.

Many people suffer from guilt and self-blame. What can be done about this?

We need to clearly examine what is our responsibility—what we have power over—and what we don't. Guilt often comes from considering something our responsibility when it isn't. For example, if we find ourselves in a dangerous situation through our own carelessness, being there is our responsibility. However, if someone physically or sexually abuses us, that isn't our responsibility. It's the other's action, not our own. Child abuse and rape aren't the responsibility of the child or the rape victim. There's no need to feel guilty or blame oneself for what happened.

If we deliberately cause another harm—for example by intentionally causing factionalism in our workplace—the pain that results is our doing. However, if we act with good intentions, and yet another experiences pain from our actions, that isn't our responsibility. For example, if we try with a kind heart to give people feedback on their actions and they get upset, that isn't our responsibility. But if we failed to take care in how we expressed ourselves, we are responsible for our miscommunication and should attempt to correct it. When we act negatively due to our own confusion and disturbing attitudes, we need not feel guilty and blame ourselves. Instead, we should try to remedy the situation as best we can and also do purification practices to counteract the negative karmic imprint on our mindstream. From the Buddhist viewpoint, guilt is a disturbing attitude: it doesn't see the situation clearly and is a form of self-centeredness. Emotionally beating up on ourselves doesn't alter the past or develop our potential. It only immobilizes us and makes us spiral downward into our own self-centeredness. On the other hand, if we have confidence in our ability to improve because we know we have the potential to become fully enlightened, we can regret our mistakes and then act to remedy the negative effects of our actions.

Buddhism emphasizes cherishing others before self. Can this lead to codependent relationships in which one person constantly sacrifices his or her own needs in order to please the other?

No, not if it is properly understood. Taking care of others can be done with two very different motivations. With one, we care for others in an unhealthy way, seemingly sacrificing ourselves, but really acting out of fear or attachment. People who are attached to praise, reputation, relationships and so forth and who fear losing these may seemingly neglect their own needs to take care of others. But in fact, they are protecting themselves in an unproductive way. Their care comes not from genuine love, but from a self-centered attempt to be happy that is actually making them more unhappy.

The other way of taking care of others is motivated by genuine affection, and this is what the Buddha encouraged.

This kind of affection and respect for others doesn't seek or expect something in return. It is rooted in the knowledge that all other beings want to be happy and to avoid pain just as much as we do. In addition, they have all benefited us either in previous lives or in this present life by doing whatever job they do in society. By steeping our minds in such thoughts, we'll naturally feel affection for others and our motivation to help them will be based on genuinely wanting them to be happy.

Codependence doesn't arise from one person in a relationship being manipulative, dependent or demanding. It evolves when two or more people's attachment, anger and fear mutually feed into each other's in unhealthy ways. If one person has cultivated nonattachment and acts with genuine love and compassion, even if another consciously or unconsciously tries to manipulate him or her, the person with clear motivation won't get hooked into a pattern of unhealthy interactions.

Can meditation solve our emotional problems?

That depends on us, our teacher and our meditation practice. In some cases it can. In others, it's more effective if people seek help from a therapist and use meditation as an adjunct.

How are Buddhism and therapy similar? How are they different?

Both seek to understand the functioning of the human mind. Both offer techniques to foster happiness and wellbeing through generating more constructive mental states. Both transmit these techniques to others through experienced guides, and both are composed of various subschools with slightly different approaches and emphases.

However, the end goals of therapy and Buddhism differ. Therapy seeks to help people be happy in this life whereas

Buddhism is concerned with their happiness in future lives and their lasting happiness through attaining liberation. Therapy doesn't regard ignorance, anger and attachment as the root causes of difficulties and therefore as attitudes to be abandoned completely. Therapists often encourage people to be angry at those who have harmed them and to find more effective ways to obtain the things they're attached to. Buddhism, on the other hand, seeks to uproot anger, attachment and selfishness from the mind altogether.

There are some differences in the methods employed in therapy and in Buddhism. Many therapies involve recollecting past traumatic experiences and reprocessing them in the present. However, Buddhism encourages students to identify their general behavior patterns and apply antidotes to them. Remembering specific childhood experiences and reliving them is not seen as important. Some therapies are concerned with the contents of the clients' dreams, whereas Buddhism generally isn't. Meditators are encouraged to identify dreams as dreams and to use the illusory nature of dream objects as an analogy to how things appear to exist independently when we're awake, while in fact they exist dependently.

The roles of spiritual masters and therapists differ as well. Therapy takes place individually or in a small group where people discuss their specific problems with the therapist. Spiritual teachers usually instruct larger groups and the students are responsible for practicing what they're taught on their own. Of course, if students need individual counseling or have questions about Dharma practice, spiritual mentors are happy to see them. Spiritual mentors are interested in how their students' meditation is progressing and in how well they're integrating it into their daily lives. One similarity I've observed is that transference may occur in relationship to either a therapist or a spiritual teacher, and depending on the awareness and level of practice of the therapist or teacher, counter-transference may also occur.

Psychology and Buddhism can learn a lot from each other, and there is increased interest in this dialogue. There is need for more research and discussion in this area.

Chapter 12

DHARMA IN DAILY LIFE

How can we live as Buddhists in modern society when its values and activities are so different from those we try to cultivate in our practice?

The more we think about the Buddha's teachings and become confident in their validity, the easier it will be to practice. For example, the more we examine our own experience and recognize the disadvantages of being attached to material possessions, the less sway advertising will have over our minds. As we see the disadvantages of unethical actions, we won't get sucked into others' unwholesome schemes. Time and effort are necessary to integrate the Buddha's teachings in our minds, but as we do it, we'll slowly progress.

Let's say we've decided to avoid taking intoxicants, and our colleagues ask us to have a drink after work. We may initially feel embarrassed and fear ridicule, but this is due to our attachment to reputation. If we are clear about what we want and don't want to do, why be afraid of others' opinions? It could be that the others drink because they feel that we expect them to, and they may be relieved when we don't! Even if they want to drink, a person who doesn't could be a good example to them. We needn't launch into a harangue against drinking, but can quietly order juice instead.

How do we tell our family and friends who aren't Buddhist about our interest in the Dharma?

At the beginning of our practice, we tend not to be sure of ourselves or very confident in the Dharma, so we are very sensitive to others' comments about what we're doing. As we gradually relax into the practice, we'll find it easier to talk with our family and colleagues about Buddhism. This doesn't mean that we should become like preachers and spew out lots of Buddhist jargon. Rather, we can answer people's questions simply, responding in a way that will make sense to them. There are many ways to talk about Buddhism without using Dharma words: after all, Buddhism is basically a commonsense approach to life. When our friends talk to us about their problems, we can discuss the antidotes to anger, jealousy or clinging in a simple way without even using the word "Buddhism."

When talking with people of other religions, we can discuss the points that Buddhism has in common with their faith. Every religion values ethics, love and compassion; so it's skillful to speak about these when first explaining Buddhism. Don't start off by talking about rebirth, karma, Buddha, Dharma, Sangha, and other unfamiliar words and concepts. Also, we can emphasize that according to Buddhism, it's very good that there's a diversity of religions because that gives people the opportunity to find a philosophy and practice that suit them. Everyone needn't become a Buddhist. This makes people of other faiths relax, because they know we respect their beliefs and won't try to convert them.

Our actions speak louder than our words. If our family notices that we're more patient and tolerant, they'll be curious about what we've done to bring about this change.

Those who are married may want to invite their spouse and children to meet their teachers or visit a Dharma center if they're interested. Some people neglect their families because they've become excited about helping all sentient beings and becoming a Buddha. They practice patience with everyone but their spouse and children, and expect the rest of the family to do all the household chores while they meditate. This isn't very skillful! While Dharma practitioners want to lessen their clinging attachment to their families, this doesn't mean they should coldly neglect them. Dharma involves generating genuine love and compassion for people we're in daily contact with, not just for sentient beings universes away whom we never see!

What can we do if our family and friends are not supportive or are even resentful of our interest in Buddhism?

First, accept that they feel that way and don't get angry about it. Being irritated at them will only increase the tension. On the other hand, we need not give up our beliefs or our practice due to family pressure. It's not wise to flaunt our practice with a rebellious attitude, but we need not hide it out of fear either. We can adapt to the external situation, while keeping our practice alive and firm internally. If our family can't relate to a shrine with pictures of the Buddha, then we can simply keep the pictures in our Dharma books and take them out when we meditate.

How do we establish a daily meditation practice and what should it include?

Set aside a clean, quiet place in your home for meditation. You can set up a small shrine there if you wish. Try to meditate at the same time each day, making the meditation sessions a comfortable length. You could start out with fifteen minutes and gradually extend it as you're able to sit longer. The mind is fresh in the morning and many people find it easier to meditate then, before the activities of the day have begun. Other people prefer to meditate in the evenings. Follow the instructions of your spiritual teacher on how to structure the sessions. You may start out with a few prayers to take refuge and set a good motivation for meditation. Then you could do some breathing meditation and, depending on your tradition, another type of meditation as well. Our meditation time is quiet time alone when we can digest our experiences, look at our lives, cultivate our good qualities, and enjoy our own company (and that of the Buddhas and bodhisattvas too!).

Must we go to the mountains and meditate to practice Dharma?

Not at all. Some people can happily remain in solitude and develop high realizations through meditation. But for a long retreat to be successful, we need to have accumulated great positive potential and to have a good foundation in the basic Dharma practices. These prerequisites can be gathered while living and practicing in society. In that way we integrate Dharma into our lives and simultaneously offer direct service to society. On the other hand, if we go to live in isolation with an emotional dream of becoming a great meditator, when in fact we can't confront our own dissatisfied mind, we'll return confused and unhappy. It's wiser to practice in a way that corresponds to our present mental state and ability.

How can we integrate Buddhism into our daily lives? How do we balance work and spiritual practice?

When you wake up in the morning, try to make your first thought, "Today, I don't want to harm anyone. I'm going to help others as much as possible. May all my actions be directed toward the long-term goal of becoming a Buddha to benefit others." After you get up, meditate for a while to get in touch with your inner calm, to learn about yourself, and to set a good motivation for the day.

During the day, be mindful of your feelings, thoughts,

words and actions. When you notice disturbing attitudes or harmful behavior, apply the antidotes taught by the Buddha. In the middle of a busy day, you can stop, breathe and get centered again before going on. Although this takes only a minute, it's sometimes hard to get ourselves to pause when we're on automatic pilot. Pausing is a good habit to develop: instead of answering the phone right away, we can think, "May I speak kindly and benefit the person on the line," and then pick up the phone. When we sit down at our desk, we can breathe quietly for a few seconds and then begin work. When we're stopped at a light or stuck in traffic, we can look around and think, "All these people around me want to be happy and to avoid problems just as I do. Because we live in an interdependent society, I receive benefit from the different jobs these people do, even though I don't know them personally." It's also very helpful to think like this when someone cuts you off!

In the evening, take a little time to review the day's events, purify your harmful behaviors, rejoice in the changes and positive attitudes you're developing, and dedicate all the positive potential for the enlightenment of all. We often expect "fast food enlightenment," not wanting to expend much time or energy to gain it. Unfortunately, things don't work that way! It's important to recognize that profound change occurs gradually. We need to rejoice at our own and others' development instead of being dissatisfied with what we haven't done.

What can we do if our practice weakens due to the influence of the external environment, and it becomes difficult to control attachment?

A daily meditation practice is an excellent remedy. In the morning we can sit quietly and spend some time remembering the disadvantages of attachment, recalling impermanence and death, and generating loving-kindness toward others. During the day, we can be aware of what we think, say and do. If we have very strong attachment toward something, it's best, as beginners, to keep some distance from it. Just as it's difficult for a fat person who is on a diet to go to a dinner party and watch everyone else eat, so too is it difficult for us to be near objects of attachment and remain unaffected. As our internal practice gets stronger and we are less drawn to superficial "glitter," we can again be with those objects and people with a peaceful mind. If our friends encourage us to go to places or do things that make our previous habitual attachment, anger, or jealousy arise, we may suggest an alternative activity or decline the invitation. If we are sincere in our practice, we will naturally make new friends with a similar interest in Dharma, and they will encourage us in a positive direction.

Chapter 13

SOCIAL ACTIVISM AND SOCIAL ISSUES

What is the Buddhist attitude toward social welfare projects?

They are necessary and very good. As Buddhists, we try to develop love and compassion for others on a mental level, but this must be expressed in action as well. His Holiness the Dalai Lama has often commented that Buddhists can learn from the Christian example of active compassion through involvement in community welfare projects. Establishing schools, hospitals, hospices, counseling services and food services for the needy directly benefits others. However, while engaging in this work, we must guard against partisanship, pride, or anger. Both our attitude and our actions must be directed toward benefiting others. Although all Buddhists need not be socially active, those who are so inclined can practice the Dharma in that context.

Does Buddhism condone social activism?

As with many questions, the answer begins with "It depends..." Depending upon our motivation and on the kind of changes we advocate and the methods we use, social activism could be helpful or harmful. Advocating policies or methods that run counter to the general Buddhist principles of nonviolence and tolerance is harmful. Even if we favor beneficial policies, if our motivation is askew, the long-term results won't be good. For example, an attitude of moral indignation that sees others in society as inept, manipulative and selfish is scarcely a constructive motivation with which to engage in social action. If we frame the situation in terms of "us versus them," and of course claim our side is right because we care for the general welfare, while theirs is wrong, then our motivation is almost identical to theirs! Such an attitude leads us to despise the "other side," and again we're caught in the cycle of attachment to what is close to the self and hatred for what is opposed.

It's important to remember that social and political problems aren't clear-cut or easily solved. Although we know this intellectually, our words and actions sometimes indicate that we seek swift and simple solutions. We must try to develop compassion for all involved parties in a conflict because they all wish to be happy and to avoid problems. For example, if we regard loggers as simply destroyers of the environment and are concerned only with stopping their harmful activities, our outlook is limited. Loggers want happiness just as we do; they also have families to support. We must value their concerns and seek solutions that contain alternative means for them to earn a living.

Should the belief in future lives make people complacent about social injustice? Does the law of karma condone oppression? Does the wish for nirvana entail ignoring the ills of this world and seeking only the bliss of liberation?

No, to all three questions. There are a variety of misconceptions: "Since there's rebirth, the poor will get another chance to be better off, therefore I don't need to help them now." "The oppressed must have created negative karma to experience such a result, and I'd be interfering with their karma if I tried to remedy their plight." "Suffering is inherent to cyclic existence. There's nothing that can be done, so I'll concern myself only with my spiritual practice, and disregard the world's ills." Such ideas reflect an incorrect understanding of karma and nirvana. Love and compassion for others are basic Buddhist principles, and acting according to them leads to liberation. The suffering in the world may be due to karma, but we can still help stop or limit it. Although lasting happiness in cyclic existence isn't possible, we can still work to lessen gross suffering and bring about relative happiness.

In fact, involvement in social action could be a means to lead others in the Dharma path. People certainly can't meditate if they're hungry. Enabling them to have food stops their gross suffering and gives them contact with kind people. This may awaken their interest in spiritual practice.

On one hand, no person is an island: we need to reach out and help each other. On the other, meditation is a solitary pursuit that is necessary to develop wisdom and compassion. Must we choose between meditation and activity, or can they be balanced?

Both are important. Meditation enables us to purify and to grow so that when we try to aid others, we'll be effective. Just as a person who wants to cure others' illnesses studies in medical school before treating patients, a person who wishes to benefit others by showing them the Dharma path must study and practice before guiding others. Meditation provides the time and space to look within and to concentrate on developing our good qualities and diminishing the harmful ones. Activity in society gives us the opportunity to act according to the understandings we've developed through meditation. Interacting with others is like the "proof of the pudding," where what we still need to work on becomes clear. In addition, actively helping others enriches our mindstreams with positive potential so that our meditation can progress.

Because each of us is unique, we will balance these two in different ways in our lives, and we may shift the balance between them from time to time, sometimes being more active, other times more contemplative. During the times we emphasize meditation, it's important to be careful that our altruism doesn't become abstract and intellectual. Similarly, while we're more active, it's important to meditate every day in order to retain a calm center from which to act.

How can we prevent burnout when we are working for others' welfare?

One way is to keep checking our motivation, continually renewing our compassionate intention. Another is to assess what we're capable of doing and to make realistic commitments. Sometimes we may be so inspired by the bodhisattva ideal that we agree to participate in every project that comes our way, even though we may lack the time or ability to complete it. Then we may push ourselves to the point of exhaustion to fulfill our commitments, or we may begin to resent those who are counting on our help. It's wise to consider before we commit, and to accept only those responsibilities that we can carry out.

In addition, we must remember that difficulties and dissatisfaction are the nature of cyclic existence. Preventing nuclear waste, dismantling apartheid, stopping the destruction of rain forests and helping the homeless are noble projects. However, even if all these goals were achieved, it wouldn't solve all the world's ills. The chief source of suffering lies in the mind: as long as ignorance, attachment and anger are present in people's minds, there will be no lasting peace on the earth. Thus, expecting our social welfare work to go smoothly, becoming attached to the results of our efforts, or thinking, "if only this would happen, the problem would be solved" leads us to become discouraged. We need to remember that in cyclic existence, there are better and worse states, but all are temporary and none bring ultimate freedom. If we are realistic, we can work in the world without expecting to bring about paradise on earth. And we can also follow our spiritual practice, knowing that it will lead to the ultimate cessation of problems.

Should we continue to try to help people who don't accept our help?

Each situation must be examined individually. First, we must check our motivation for helping others. Is it because we think we know what's best for "this person who can't get his life together?" Is it because we want to feel needed? If we have such attitudes, we're likely to try to force our advice on others, which will cause them to recoil.

We must also examine whether we've acted skillfully, or whether our help has undermined others' sense of self-esteem. We can also check their receptivity, for sometimes we may act in good faith and with skill, but others aren't receptive to our efforts. In situations like these, it's best to stop actively trying to help but to still keep the door of communication open so that if they change later, they'll feel comfortable contacting us again. Stomping away from situations in which we've unsuccessfully tried to help and complaining, "See how much I've done for you and you don't appreciate it!" increases others' resentment and prevents them from seeking our aid in the future. Sometimes acceptance, patience and inaction are the most effective ways we can be of aid.

Does Buddhism give guidelines for protection of the environment?

Yes. Interdependence, protection of life and loving-kindness are three of the Buddha's most important teachings. Interdependence refers to the interrelationship of phenomena. In this case, sentient beings and the environment depend upon each other for survival, and thus it's in the interest of human beings to protect the environment. Traditionally, Buddhists advocate nonviolence and the protection of life. Because humans, animals and insects are all life-forms, Buddhism advocates the preservation of endangered species. In addition, as an expression of loving-kindness for ourselves, future generations and all beings, Buddhism stresses the protection not only of the earth on which all of us depend, but also the protection of all sentient life on it.

Attachment is one of the chief causes of humankind's exploitation of the environment. Craving for more and better causes us to take all we can from the earth and to ignore the long-term consequences of doing this. If we lessen our attachment by developing contentment with what we have, we will be able to live more in harmony with our environment and the other beings who share it with us.

Are Buddhists concerned about the environment?

They need to be! Unfortunately in Asia, many people lack education on this subject. Even in the West, where environmental issues make the headlines, some Buddhists neglect easy ways, such as recycling, to protect the environment. Taking care about how we dispose of our cans, jars and paper is part of the practice of mindfulness in our homes! Compassion and concern for others should motivate us to minimize the use of disposable, nonrecyclable materials in temples and Dharma centers and to recycle the materials we can.

A significant number of Western and Asian Buddhists are concerned about the environment and are involved in socially engaged projects. The Buddhist Peace Fellowship (Box 4650, Berkeley CA 94704) is noteworthy and can supply reading lists, addresses of socially engaged Buddhist organizations worldwide, and back issues of their excellent journal. *The Path of Compassion,* edited by Fred Eppsteiner and published by Parallax Press, provides a Buddhist perspective on social engagement.

What does Buddhism say about animal rights?

Buddhism regards animals as living beings who experience pleasure and pain and who cherish their own lives just as humans do. Therefore, Buddhism would not advocate putting homeless cats and dogs to sleep. Nor would it condone cruel experimentation on animals or the dreadful living conditions of animals raised for slaughter. Although theoretically Buddhism favors vegetarianism, practically speaking, many Buddhists do not keep this.

Why do people in some Buddhist traditions eat meat, while those in others are vegetarian?

Initially, it may seem confusing that the Theravadins of Sri Lanka and Southeast Asia eat meat, the Chinese Mahayanists do not, the Japanese Mahayanists do, and the Tibetans, who practice the Vajrayana, do. This difference depends on the different emphasis of each tradition: Theravadin teachings emphasize eliminating attachment toward sense objects and the discriminating mind that says, "I like this and not that." Thus, when the monks go out to collect alms, they are to accept silently and with gratitude whatever is offered to them, be it meat or not. If a monk were to say, "I can't eat meat, so give me more of those delicious vegetables," it would offend the benefactors as well as harm his own practice of nonattachment, Thus, provided that the meat comes from an animal that the monk neither kills himself, orders to be killed, nor sees, hears or suspects is killed to give him the meat, he is permitted to eat it. However, those who offer food to the Sangha should remember that the principal premise of Buddhism is not to harm others and should choose what they offer accordingly. Upon the basis of nonattachment, the Mahayana tradition emphasizes compassion for other beings. Thus, a practitioner of this tradition is advised not to eat meat in order to avoid inflicting pain on any being and to prevent potential butchers from committing negative actions. Also, the ignorant, lusty or aggressive energy of an animal can affect an ordinary practitioner who eats its flesh, thus impeding his or her development of great compassion. Therefore, vegetarianism is recommended. The Chinese Mahayana monks and nuns are strict vegetarians while the laypeople generally eat meat.

Although Japanese Buddhism is Mahayana, both the priests and the laypeople generally eat meat. This is due to the geography of Japan, where people have for centuries depended on the sea for the source of their food.

The tantric path or Vajrayana has four classes. In the lower classes, external cleanliness and purity are emphasized as techniques to help the practitioner generate internal purity of mind. Therefore, these practitioners do not eat meat, which is regarded as impure. On the other hand, in the highest yoga tantra, on the basis of nonattachment and compassion, a qualified practitioner meditates on the subtle nervous system. For this, one's bodily elements need to be very strong, and thus eating meat is recommended for such a person. Also, this class of tantra stresses the transformation of ordinary objects through meditation on selflessness. Such practitioners, by virtue of their profound meditation, are not greedily eating meat for their own pleasure.

In Tibet, there is an additional factor to consider: due to the high altitude and harsh climate, there is little to eat besides ground barley, dairy products and meat. The people had to eat meat to stay alive. His Holiness the Dalai Lama has encouraged the Tibetans living in exile in countries where vegetables and fruits are more plentiful to refrain from eating meat whenever possible.

If practitioners suffer severe health problems, their spiritual masters sometimes encourage them to eat meat. In this way, they can keep their bodies healthy to use it for Dharma practice.

The Buddha prohibited all of his followers—ordained and lay—from eating meat under three circumstances: (1) when they kill the animal themselves, (2) when they ask another person to kill it for them, or (3) when they know or suspect that someone killed the animal to feed to them. By avoiding meat obtained in any of these three ways, people do not create the negative action of killing. The question then arises, "What about eating meat bought at the market?" Many teachers say that is permissible. My personal opinion is that some karma must be involved simply because consumer demand creates the supply of meat, which entails the taking of lives. However, this karma would be different from that created by directly killing the animal oneself.

It's better if those who eat meat eat the flesh of large animals. This minimizes the number of lives that are taken to provide a meal. Only one cow need lose its life to provide many people with several meals, whereas many shrimp must die to give one person only one meal. People who eat meat are also encouraged to develop a sense of gratitude and compassion for the animals who have given their lives so they can eat. In this way, they will aspire to practice the Dharma well to "repay" the kindness of the animals. Also, non-vegetarians can recite the mantra *om ahbirakay tsara hung* seven times over the meat and pray for the animal to have a fortunate rebirth.

We can't brand people as "good Buddhists" or "bad Buddhists" by looking at their dinner plates. Those who eat meat with a sense of gratitude and compassion for the animal may be more spiritual than "fundamentalist vegetarians" who are intolerant of anything but their own view. Each person must check his or her own level of practice, bodily requirements and the food source in their environment and eat accordingly, without insisting that everyone else eat as he or she does. It isn't what we eat that makes us enlightened, it's what we do with our minds.

Is organ donation considered beneficial according to Buddhism?

In general, offering parts of one's body for the benefit of others is virtuous. Nowadays this is much easier than in the past because a kidney, for example, can frequently be transplanted from one person to another without great complications. However, each case must be regarded separately, depending on one's motivation and the other's condition.

Donating one's organs after death is a choice that will vary from person to person, depending on each individual's state of mind and level of spiritual practice. In some cases, removing organs after the heart has stopped but before the consciousness has left could interrupt the death process and be detrimental. In others, the force of the person's compassion and wish to benefit others can override any inconvenience that person may experience and could be an ultimate act of caring for others. It's a personal decision.

What is the Buddhist view on abortion?

According to Buddhism, the consciousness joins with the fertilized egg at the moment of conception, and thus the fetus is a living being. However, unwanted pregnancy is a difficult situation, and we must think creatively about how to help people in that situation. There is no black-and-white answer; each situation is unique. But no matter what choice is made, the pain can't be denied.

Currently, there is great debate in America about abortion, and both sides claim to be right. However, I see much anger and very little compassion in both camps. Yet, compassion for the parents and the child involved in an unwanted pregnancy is what is needed. We are put in the situation of looking for the "best" solution in cases where there are no good solutions, and we must consider both the short- and long-term effects on both the parents and the child. For example, abortion may terminate the pregnancy and solve the immediate problem, but the parents may have unresolved emotions afterward, and the karma they and the doctor create will adversely influence their future happiness. Better education and counseling about birth control, especially for teenagers, is needed. Young people also need realistic education about romance. But to teach that, adults must first develop it! And that means dismantling the many fairy tales and Hollywood stories we grew up with. Also, we can improve adoption services: there are many childless couples who would like children. I appreciate the choice that the natural parents of my adopted relatives and friends made. Without it, I would never have known those people who are now very dear to me.

Is birth control allowed in Buddhism?

Yes, depending on the method. Birth control methods that prevent conception are permitted. However, once conception has taken place and consciousness has entered the fertilized egg, it's a different situation. Thus morning-after pills and other such methods are discouraged.

What is the Buddhist view on the death penalty?

Life is the most valuable possession any person has, even if that person acts in a criminal manner. Buddhism recommends rehabilitation or imprisonment rather than execution. The proper motivation is needed for imprisoning others, however. That is, imprisonment is to protect a person from harming others and from creating more negative karma that would bring him or her misery later. Seeking revenge or feeling glee at punishing others are opposite to the kind heart that Buddhism encourages us to develop.

Is self-defense ever justifiable in light of the Buddhist emphasis on non-violence?

Self-defense needn't involve violence, and nonviolence doesn't mean becoming a doormat. We can seek ways to protect ourselves from harm without harming others or by inflicting the least amount of harm necessary. With however much time is available, we can try to diminish our self-centeredness and reflect on compassion before acting.

Someone who cherishes others more than him- or herself would generally choose to give up his or her own life rather than to slay another. There is a story about a general who was furious with a monk who refused to answer a question. Drawing his sword, the general shouted, "Do you know I could stick this into you without thinking twice?" The monk calmly replied, "And do you know I could have it stuck in me without thinking twice?" If we are unattached to our bodies and do not want to take the lives of others, we may be willing to give up our own lives.

However, most of us are not capable of doing that with a happy mind. If we feel we cannot avoid killing, we can at least try to do it not with glee, but with regret at having to cause another pain. If our intention to cause harm is weak, the karmic effect of the act will be less.

What can we do in times of war or if someone threatens our loved ones?

It's best to seek other ways to handle difficult situations without resorting to violence. If we use our intelligence and creativity, we could probably find other solutions. Surely diplomacy is more effective than war. No matter how difficult our situation, we always have a choice of how to act. We can distract or injure someone rather than kill him or her. If there is a war, we can consider carefully what choice to make. We can weigh the advantages and disadvantages of killing and not killing in this and in future lives, and the effects of this action on ourselves and others. Then we can decide according to what we consider best (or least harmful!), although there may be no easy solution.

What can we do about insects in our house?

We can be creative in the way we remove them! It's not necessary to kill them. It may take a bit more time to put an ant on a piece of paper and carry it outside, or to catch a spider or cockroach in a plastic container and take it away, but when we consider the consequences of killing and that each small insect cherishes its life just as we cherish ours, we won't mind the extra effort.

Is killing ever permissible?

There is a story about Shakyamuni Buddha in a previous life when, as a bodhisattva, he was the captain of a ship. He knew that the oarsman was going to kill and rob the five hundred merchants on board. He had intense compassion not only for the victims, but also for the oarsman, who would experience the torturous karmic results of killing. In addition, he was willing to take upon himself any negative karmic effects of killing. He thus decided to kill the oarsman, but because his motivation was so pure, the karmic effect of killing was minimal and he created great positive potential.

Chapter 14

WOMEN AND THE DHARMA

Can both men and women attain liberation and enlightenment?

Views on this differ among the various Buddhist traditions. According to the Vajrayana, both women and men equally can attain liberation and enlightenment. However, the Theravada and general Mahayana presentations say that although one can attain liberation with a female body, to attain full enlightenment one has to have a male body in the very last rebirth.

A Buddha is beyond being either male or female. An enlightened being can manifest in any type of body—human or animal, male or female—that is beneficial for sentient beings. Looking closer, we can ask, "Is our present mind male or female?" When we watch our breath or observe our mind in meditation, is there anything about our mind that is male or female? Or are those terms that are designated according to the arrangement of the atoms forming our bodies? Do we make "male" and "female" more solid and inherently existent than they actually are?

Can women make offerings and prayers during menstruation? Can they meditate at that time?

Of course! Any notion that they can't is superstition.

Is it harder for a woman to practice the Dharma than for a man?

That depends on the individual. For some women, their menstrual cycle causes many emotional changes. But they can learn to deal with them. After all, men can be moody too! I believe that the principal thing that holds a woman back is if she has a limited self-concept and lack of self-confidence due to societal values or family upbringing. If we think we can't do something well, then we don't even try. What a waste of human potential! As long as we are human beings with human intelligence, and have not only met the Dharma but also have all the necessary conditions to practice and attain realizations, then let's do it! The success of our practice depends on our own self-confidence and effort, not on others' opinions. Historically, many women have attained liberation and enlightenment: we can read their stories in the *Therigatha*, in some of the Mahayana sutras and in tantric biographies.

Have women participated as equals in Buddhist institutions?

In most Western and Asian cultures, women's activities have been more restricted and their social position lower than men's. The position and opportunities open to women in Western society have undergone much change in recent years, but haven't changed as much in Asia. In the sixth century B.C. when the Buddha was alive, women were considered subordinate to men, and their societal roles were very restricted. Conforming with Indian values, the Buddha designated that the nuns sit behind the monks and be served after them, and that the nuns' community be under the care of the monks. This is due to the societal customs of ancient India, and is not indicative of women's intelligence or capability. In fact, while the male is representative of the method aspect of the path to enlightenment, the female is symbolic of the wisdom aspect!

Although it's said that the Buddha initially refused to admit women into the monastic order, he soon consented to fully ordain women and to establish the nuns' community. These were revolutionary steps according to ancient Indian society. At that time, women were considered the property of first their fathers, then their husbands and finally their sons. That the Buddha clearly recognized women's potential to attain liberation and encouraged them in their practice by giving them full ordination is remarkable given the society in which he lived. Aside from the Jains, Buddhism was the only religion at that time to ordain women.

Although women's capability to practice the Dharma and attain high realizations has traditionally been recognized, women have occupied second place in Buddhist institutions due to cultural prejudice. However, internal practice is very different from external power and recognition. A true practitioner is more concerned with the former than the latter. That doesn't mean, however, that women must complacently accept institutionalized cultural biases. We must work to remedy them, motivated not by pride or anger, but because we want all beings—men and women alike—to be able to practice well and attain enlightenment.

In Buddhism, there are different levels of ordination—eight-precept holder, novice (*sramanerika*) or fully ordained nun (*bhikshuni*). The level of ordination available to women differs from one country to another and this influences how various Asian societies regard their ordained female practitioners. Among the Chinese, the nuns can take full ordination. Educated and active in society, many are spiritual masters themselves. Chinese nuns currently outnumber the monks. In contrast, the full ordination for women isn't available in Thailand, and the women who have taken eight precepts have an ambiguous status between lay and ordained. In Sri Lanka, women may take ten percepts, and they have a similar ambiguous status. Among the Tibetans, the novice ordination for women is available, but the lineage of the full ordination did not spread to Tibet. Although there have been several great female practitioners in Tibet, few Tibetan women currently teach the Dharma.

Women from Buddhist traditions that lack the lineage for women's full ordination are now interested in instituting this ordination in their tradition. Both monks and nuns are studying to determine how to transmit the ordination lineage from one tradition to another. Some women, both Asian and Western, have already gone to Taiwan, Hong Kong or the U.S.A. to take the full ordination in Chinese or Korean temples.

As Buddhism comes to the West, I believe that cultural biases against women will be left behind because present Western cultures won't tolerate them. At present in the West, women are very active in Buddhist organizations and often are leaders or teachers. However, because sexual discrimination still exists, we must be vigilant and ensure that biases against women don't creep into Buddhist translations, rituals or education in the West.

There have recently been two international conferences for Buddhist women, and interest in improving all aspects of life for female practitioners is increasing. It's inspiring to see women from various cultures and traditions unite in their common aspiration to practice and actualize the Buddha's teachings.

Chapter 15

MONKS, NUNS, LAY PRACTITIONERS AND SPIRITUAL TEACHERS

What does taking ordination as a monk or nun entail?

Ordination involves taking certain precepts or vows set out by the Buddha and making an effort to live according to them. It is founded upon making a commitment to steer our physical, verbal and mental energies in productive directions instead of indiscriminately acting out any thought that comes into our minds. Lay people can also take vows that are called the five lay precepts: to abandon killing, stealing, unwise sexual behavior, lying and intoxicants.

When people decide that they would like to become a monk or nun or to take the five lay precepts, they request their teacher. If the teacher feels that they have a proper foundation, he or she will arrange the ordination ceremony.

What are the benefits of taking ordination as a monk or nun? Is it necessary to practice the Dharma?

No, it isn't necessary to become a monk or nun to practice the Dharma. Taking ordination is an individual choice that each person must make for him- or herself. Historically, many lay men and women have gained high realizations. It's inspiring to learn about their lives and to emulate them. Ordination isn't suitable for everyone.

However, there are some advantages to being ordained: by living within the precepts, one is constantly accumulating positive potential. As long as ordained people aren't breaking the precepts, they are continuously enriching their mindstreams with positive potential even when they're asleep. They have more time for practice and encounter fewer distractions: family obligations can consume much time and energy. Children require a lot of attention, and it's difficult to meditate if they are playing or crying nearby. People who see these things as distractions and who want to pacify their minds and accumulate a rich store of positive potential may decide to take ordination to have a more conducive situation for practice.

How can a lay person practice the Dharma?

Lay men and women can practice the Dharma by subduing their minds. In some Buddhist cultures, some people downgrade their potential by thinking, "I'm a lay person. Listening to teachings, chanting and meditating are the work of monks and nuns. It's not my job. I just go to the temple, bow, make offerings and pray for the welfare of my family." These activities are good, but lay people are capable of a much richer spiritual life, in terms of both learning Buddhism and integrating it into their daily life. It's important to attend Dharma talks and to follow a series of talks if possible. By doing this, lay people will understand the real truth and beauty of the Dharma. Otherwise, they will remain "joss stick Buddhists" (people who go to the temple and offer joss stick incense with much ceremony and little understanding), and if someone asks them a question about Buddhism, they'll have difficulty in responding. That is a sad situation. However, I've noticed that many young lay Asian Buddhists and Western Buddhists are eager to meditate and study the Dharma. This is very good.

It's very beneficial for lay Buddhists to take the five lay precepts for the duration of their life or take eight precepts (the five plus three more) on special days, such as new and full moon days. In this way, they increase their practice of mindfulness as well as create much positive potential. In addition, they can attend weekend retreats and teachings at temples and Dharma centers or use some of their annual vacation time to go on longer retreats.

Responsibility for the existence and dissemination of the Buddha's teachings lies with the monks, nuns and lay people. If we value the Buddha's teachings and want them to continue to exist and to flourish, then we have the responsibility to learn and practice them ourselves according to our capabilities.

Do people become monks and nuns to escape the harsh realities of life?

If people become monks or nuns for this reason, their motivation is impure and they will not find ordained life satisfying. The causes of suffering—attachment, ignorance and hatred—follow us everywhere. They don't need a passport to go with us to another country, nor are they left outside the monastery gates. If all we had to do to escape the hassles of life was to shave our head and put on robes, I think everyone would do it! But unfortunately, it's not that easy. As long as we have attachment, ignorance and hatred, we can't escape problems be we ordained or lay.

People who ask this question think that having a job, a mortgage and a family are difficult tasks and constitute the "harsh reality of life." But it is a much harsher reality to be honest with ourselves and to recognize our own mistaken conceptions and harmful behavior. It is a harder job to work on eliminating our anger, attachment and closed-mindedness. People who meditate and pray may not be able to show a skyscraper or a paycheck as the sign of their success, but that doesn't mean that they're lazy and irresponsible. It takes a great deal of effort to change our detrimental habits of body, speech and mind; it's not easy to become a Buddha. Instead of "escaping" reality, sincere practitioners are trying to discover it! Chasing after sense pleasures, distracting ourselves through watching television, shopping or drinking are ways of escaping reality, for these activities distract us from looking at the reality of death and the functioning of cause and effect. In the Dharma sense, this is laziness, because no effort is being made to subdue our attachment, anger and closed-mindedness.

Some people think, "Only people who can't make it in the 'real world' become monks and nuns. Maybe they have family problems, or they didn't do well in school, or they can't get a good job. They live in the temple and take vows just to have a home and an occupation." Should people seek ordination for this reason, they lack the proper motivation, and the masters who give ordination need to weed such people out. On the contrary, those who take ordination with a correct motivation have strong aspiration to develop their potential, to subdue their minds and to help others.

Do all monks and nuns take the vow to be celibate, or may they marry?

All monks and nuns take a vow to be celibate. In Japan, the tradition of lay priests developed. These people don't take vows of celibacy and may marry. Some priests shave their heads and wear robes, others don't.

In Tibetan Buddhism, one may be a lay person with a family and still be a spiritual teacher. Out of respect for the Dharma, such teachers sometimes wear clothes that resemble monastic robes, but aren't. This is sometimes confusing for people who can't tell the difference in the clothes and wonder why a "monk" or "nun" has long hair. Thus, His Holiness the Dalai Lama recently asked these practitioners to add a white band to their shawls to indicate that they are lay, not monastic, practitioners.

Can someone be ordained for a short period of time, or must it be for one's entire life?

This differs in each Buddhist tradition. In Thailand, a man may become a monk for a few weeks or months and then return to lay life. Most young men in Thailand do this, and it's considered an honor for his family. In the Chinese and Tibetan traditions, ordination is taken for life. However, if a person is unhappy being ordained and later wants to leave the order, he or she may return the vows and resume lay life.

What is the relationship between the sangha (ordained monks and nuns) and lay practitioners?

As the Buddha designed it, the sangha's responsibility was to keep their vows, learn and practice the Dharma, and teach and guide the lay people. The lay people in turn were to provide the requisites for life: housing, clothes, food and medicine. This system gave the ordained practitioners more time to study and meditate, so they could progress along the path and thus be able to guide others in the society more effectively. This relationship has continued to some extent in all the Buddhist traditions, although in various forms. In the Chinese Ch'an (Zen) tradition, work is valued as part of the practice, and monks and nuns tend the fields as well as study and meditate. In Thailand, the vow not to handle money is strictly kept, and the lay people not only provide everything the sangha needs, but do a lot of the manual work in the monasteries. In Asia, monks and nuns are generally respected and cared for because those societies value Dharma practice. However, they should consider themselves the servants of others, and not become proud when they receive offerings or respect. If they do, their own practice will decline. In the West the relationship between ordained and lay practitioners is still in its formative stages. In general it tends to be less formal or hierarchical than in Asia. However, the financial needs of Western ordained sangha are not always provided by a monastery, center or other organization. Some Western monks and nuns are forced to don lay clothes and find jobs to support themselves. Some have friends and relatives who support them, others teach and receive offerings. The financial situation for Western monks and nuns is often difficult.

When people take ordination, do they reject their family and friends?

Not at all. They aren't rejecting their families and friends simply because they've decided not to live a family life themselves. Although they wish to give up their attachment to their family and friends, ordained people still appreciate the kindness of their family and friends and reflect this in their wish to make the world a better place through their religious practice. Rather than limiting their affection and care to the people they are close to, ordained people seek to develop impartial love for all and to consider all beings as part of their family.

Monks and nuns believe that by purifying and developing their minds, they'll be able to guide others to lasting happiness through the Dharma. They know this is of great benefit not only to their families but also to society as a whole. Even if they do not attain high realizations in this lifetime, they have a broad vision and work for long-range happiness and benefit. They think, "If I continue with my worldly life, my disturbing attitudes will surface and I'll harm others as well as create the cause for my own unfortunate rebirth. How can I help my family and all others if I do that? But if I practice the Dharma, my own qualities will increase and I'll be able to help them better."

How can parents view their child's becoming a monk or nun?

They can be very happy. It's a sign that they have done a good job as parents by instilling in their child a sense of ethics and care for others. Some parents become upset if their child wants to become a monk or nun. They fear that he or she won't be happy or won't be financially secure. Some parents are angry: "We paid so much for your education. Who will take care of us when we're old if you're in a monastery?" Parents with this attitude mean well: they want their child to be happy. But having a family, career and many possessions isn't the only way to happiness. Of course, when Shakyamuni Buddha left his luxurious life at the palace to seek the lasting happiness of enlightenment, his parents were upset too! But parents who understand the Dharma will want their child to be happy now and in the future, and they'll understand that religious practice is a way to bring that about. They'll rejoice that their child is devoting him or herself to the noble goals of the Dharma.

Is taking ordination a painful sacrifice?

It shouldn't be. Ordained people shouldn't feel, "I really want to do these things, but now I have vows and can't." If they do feel this way, they won't be happy being ordained. Abandoning negative actions should be seen not as a burden but as a joy. Such an attitude comes from contemplating cause and effect.

When we take vows, whether they are the five precepts of a lay person or the vows of a monk or nun, we first generate the attitude, "In my heart, I really don't want to kill, steal, lie and so on." Sometimes we may be weak in an actual situation and may feel tempted to do these things, but taking precepts gives us extra strength and determination not to do what we really don't want to do. We'll find more strength to avert the disturbing attitudes that could cause us to act negatively. In this way, precepts are liberating, not confining, for they help us free ourselves from habitual, unwholesome tendencies.

Is it necessary to have a spiritual teacher? How do we find one?

It's very helpful. We can get some information from books, but a teacher can answer our questions and provide an example of how to integrate the teachings into our lives. To find a spiritual teacher, we can attend teachings given by various people and gradually decide. We can have more than one teacher, although one of them usually becomes our principal, or root, teacher.

We should seek qualified teachers. This is especially important given that there's such a spiritual supermarket in the West. Qualified teachers act ethically, have sound meditative experience, and correctly understand emptiness. They have also studied the Buddhist scriptures in depth, are able to teach a variety of Dharma subjects, and have a good relationship with their own teachers. They are motivated to teach out of genuine concern for their students, not out of desire for offerings and fame. They are compassionate and patient and will try to help their students no matter how many mistakes the students may make.

How do we relate to our teachers?

We benefit from recognizing our teachers' good qualities and treating them with respect; respecting others opens us to benefit from their guidance. Also, it's helpful if we provide for our teachers and help them with tasks that need to be done. When our teachers give us Dharma instructions either in a large group or privately, we benefit by putting what we've learned into practice as best we can.

Respecting our teachers and following their guidance doesn't mean allowing ourselves to get into unhealthy relationships with them. Some people talk about "surrendering" to the spiritual guide. What is to be surrendered is our egocentric disturbing attitudes, not our wisdom, common sense and responsibility for our own lives. Also, it's inappropriate to dote on our teachers, or to become possessive of them and jealous of other students. Our teachers' role is to guide us to enlightenment, not to fulfill all our emotional needs. Spiritual teachers are not substitutes for parents or therapists.

Sometimes we encounter Buddhists, both lay and ordained, who are ill-natured and difficult to get along with despite their religious practice. Why is this so?

Not all Buddhists are already Buddhas! Some don't take the Buddha's guidance on ethical matters seriously. And even those who do must spend a long time transforming their minds. Dissolving anger isn't an easy process. We can understand this from our own experience: when we are in the habit of losing our temper, it takes more than just saying "I shouldn't do this" for us to stop. It calls for consistent and correct practice. We have to be patient with ourselves, and similarly, we need to be patient with others. We're all fighting the same internal enemies—disturbing attitudes and imprints of past actions. Sometimes we're strong in confronting them, other times we're carried away by anger, jealousy, attachment or pride. It does no good to judge or blame ourselves when we succumb to the disturbing attitudes. Likewise, blaming and criticizing others when they do so is fruitless. Knowing how difficult it is to transform ourselves, we should also be patient with others.

The fact that all practitioners aren't perfect doesn't mean

the method taught by the Buddha is imperfect. It means either they don't practice it well or their practice is not yet strong enough. It's extremely important that we try to be harmonious and to accept each others' weaknesses. Our job isn't to point fingers and say, "Why don't you practice better? Why don't you control your temper?" Our job is to ask ourselves, "Why don't I practice better so their actions won't make me angry?" and "What can I do to help them?"

What can we think and do if we see a spiritual teacher or someone who is ordained act in a way that seems inappropriate to us?

We must first develop a constructive attitude ourselves, and then determine a proper course of action. It's not healthy to whitewash seemingly inappropriate behavior, nor does it help ourselves or others to become indignant and raise a ruckus. It's natural to feel disappointed when someone we respect acts in a way that seems inappropriate. But it's important to ask ourselves, "Am I disappointed and angry because that person isn't what I want them to be? Or am I sad because perhaps that person is having difficulties and needs help?" There's a big difference in the two attitudes: the first is self-centered—we are upset because someone we set up as an idol or role model isn't acting in the way we expect and want. The other is compassionate and seeks to benefit the person. It's beneficial to examine the expectations we have of others and to cultivate the latter attitude.

The next step is to think about how best to help in the situation. Each situation is different. In some cases, we can approach the person directly and ask about the behavior. In other situations, we may feel it's best to speak to the person's teacher or Dharma friends. Some situations can be resolved quietly, others may require public discussion. In any case, it helps us to cultivate an attitude that is honest and compassionate—not accusatory, hurt or self-righteous.

Chapter 16

FAMILY AND CHILDREN

How can Buddhism help our family life?

Family harmony is extremely important, and divorce is traumatic for parents and children alike. If adults see the main purpose of marriage as pleasure, then arguments and the breakup of the family come about more easily. As soon as people don't get as much pleasure as they want, discontent sets in, quarrels ensue and the marriage collapses. Many people go on to have numerous partners, but still fail to find satisfaction. This is a clear example of the way in which clinging to one's own pleasure brings pain to oneself and others.

It's helpful for partners to hold the Dharma as the center of their relationship. That is, both partners are determined to live ethically and to develop their loving-kindness toward all beings impartially. If two people communicate well together, they can help each other to do this: when one partner becomes discouraged or starts to neglect the practice, they can discuss it and the other can help. If they have children, they can help each other have time for quiet reflection and time with the children. Children aren't antithetical to Dharma practice! Parents can learn a lot about themselves from their children and they can help each other work through the challenges of parenthood in the light of Buddhist values.

Influenced by contemporary trends in psychology, many people have come to attribute most of their problems to childhood experiences in their family of origin. However, if this is done with an attitude of blame—"I have problems because of what my parents did or didn't do when I was a child"—then it sets the stage for those same people to feel guilty and fearful that they will damage their own children once they have families. This kind of anxiety is scarcely conducive to healthy childrearing or to feeling compassion for ourselves. It's damaging to ourselves and our children if we view our own childhood as if it were an illness we have to recover from!

Although we can't ignore detrimental influences from childhood, it's just as important to pay attention to the kindness and benefit we have received from our families. No matter what our situation was when we were growing up, we were the recipients of much kindness from others. It's essential to remember this and to let ourselves feel the gratitude that naturally arises. If we do, we also can pass that same kindness and care on to our children.

How can the Dharma help children? How can we teach it to them?

The essence of the Buddha's teaching is to cease harming others and to help them as much as possible. These are values that both Buddhist and non-Buddhist parents want to instill in their children so that they can live harmoniously with others. Since children learn largely through example, the most effective way for parents to teach their children Buddhist values is to live them themselves. Of course, this isn't always so easy! But if parents try to practice well, their children will directly benefit from their example.

It's helpful for children to grow up with Buddhism in their home. If a family has a shrine in the home, the children can keep it tidy and make offerings. One friend and her three-year-old daughter bow to the Buddha three times every morning. The child then gives the Buddha a present—some fruit or cookies—and the Buddha gives one back to the child (usually the previous day's offering). Children love music, and the melodies of prayers, mantras and Buddhist songs can take the place of the usual commercial jingles and nursery rhymes. I know several couples who chant mantras to their babies when the infants are upset or sleepy, and they react to the gentle vibration. Another family I know offers their food before every meal and their five-year-old son leads the prayer. These are simple yet profound ways for parents and children to share spirituality.

Several Buddhist families could gather together on a weekly or monthly basis to practice together. Rather than just taking the kids to Sunday School and letting someone else teach them, practicing together provides the opportunity for the parents and children to spend some peaceful time together apart from their harried schedules. It also enables Buddhist families to meet and support each other. Activities for young children could include singing Buddhist songs, prayers and mantras, learning to bow to the Buddha and make offerings at the shrine, and doing a short breathing meditation. Parents and school-age children could role-play together, creating a scene in which all the characters think of their own happiness above others' and then replaying it with one of the characters thinking of others' happiness. Such activities teach children problem-solving and let them see the results of different behaviors. Families could also visit Buddhist temples and centers together on outings.

Reading Buddhist children's books and watching Buddhist videos are other activities parents can share with their children. There is an excellent cartoon video of the Buddha's life, and several children's Dharma books. Informal discussions with children can be both amusing and instructive: children are open to concepts such as rebirth, karma, kindness to animals and so forth.

Discussion groups work well with teenagers. An adult can facilitate a discussion about friendship or other subjects of concern to teenagers. The beauty of Buddhism is that its principles can apply to every aspect of life. The more children see the relevance of ethical values and loving-kindness to their lives, the more they will value those traits. Once I led a discussion group of about twenty teenagers about boy-girl relationships. Each person spoke in turn, and although they were ostensibly talking about their lives and feelings, there was a lot of Dharma in what they said. For example, they brought out the importance of living ethically. As the facilitator, I didn't teach or preach; I just listened and respected what they said. Afterward some of them came up to me and said, "Wow! That's the first time we've ever talked about that with a nun!" Not only were they able to talk openly in the presence of an adult about a sensitive topic, but they also understood that religious people aren't unaware of teenagers' concerns.

What if our children aren't interested in Buddhism? Should we allow them to go to church with their friends?

Religion should not be forced on anyone. If children aren't interested in Buddhism, let them be. They can still learn how to be a kind person from observing their parents' attitudes and actions.

Classmates are likely to invite our children to go to church with them. Because we live in a multicultural and multi-religious society, it's helpful for children to learn about other traditions by attending their friends' church or temple. When they do so, we should prepare them by discussing the fact that people have different beliefs, and thus mutual respect and tolerance are important. Our children can also invite their classmates to a Dharma center or some Buddhist activities, thus promoting mutual learning and respect.

How can we introduce children to meditation?

Children are often curious when they see their parents do their daily meditation practice. This can be an opportunity to teach them a simple breathing meditation. Children enjoy sitting quietly alongside their parents for five or ten minutes. When their attention span sags, they can quietly get up and go in another room while the parents continue to meditate. If parents find this too disturbing, they can do their daily practice privately and meditate together with their youngsters at another time.

Children can also learn visualization meditation. Most children love to pretend and can easily imagine things. Parents can teach their children to imagine the Buddha, made of light. Then, while light radiates from the Buddha into them and all the beings around them, they can chant the Buddha's mantra. If a child has a sick relative, friend or pet, or if a friend is having problems, the child could visualize that person specifically and imagine the Buddha sending light to him or her.

Dharma centers usually schedule events for adults and no childcare is provided. What can we do?

Dharma centers need to gradually expand their range of activities. Parents who are members could meet together and discuss how to do this, utilizing some of the suggestions above. They then can organize family activities or activities for children at the centers.

How can we have good relationships with our children, especially when they're teenagers?

Having an open relationship with teenagers is important, and this depends on how the parents relate to their children when they're small. This, in turn, depends on spending time with the children and on having a positive attitude toward them. When parents are harried, they tend to see having children as a hassle—yet another thing to take care of before they can collapse. Children pick up on this and it influences them. Building good relationships with children depends on setting priorities. It may mean accepting a job that pays less but has shorter hours or turning down a promotion that would have increased family income but meant more stress and less time at home. Love is more important than material possessions to children. Choosing to earn more money at the expense of good family relations may mean later having to spend that extra income on therapy and counseling for both parents and children!

Do children need discipline? How do we do that without getting angry?

Children often provide the best—and the most difficult—opportunity to practice patience! It's helpful if parents become familiar with the antidotes to anger taught by the Buddha (see "Working with Anger" in this book). However, patience doesn't mean letting children do whatever they want to. That is, in fact, being cruel to children, for it allows them to develop bad habits which make it more difficult for them to get along with others. Children need guidelines and limits; they need to learn the results of different behaviors, and how to discriminate which to practice and which to abandon.

Contentment is an essential Buddhist principle. How can we teach it to children?

I believe one source of difficulty lies in giving children so much choice about their sense pleasures. From a young age, they are asked, "Do you want apple juice or orange juice? Do you want to watch this TV show or that one? Do you want this kind of bicycle or that? Do you want a red toy or a green one?" It seems to me that children get confused by being bombarded with so many choices. Instead of learning to be content with whatever they have, they are constantly forced to think, "Which thing will bring me the most happiness? What else can I get to make me happy?" This increases their greed and confusion. Remedying this doesn't mean that parents become authoritarian. Rather, they can place less emphasis on the importance of these things in the home. Of course, this also depends on parents' altering the ways they themselves relate to sense pleasure and material possessions. If parents cultivate contentment, their children will find it easier to do so as well.

Chapter 17

SHRINES AND OFFERINGS

What is the purpose of a shrine? What is put on it?

A shrine reminds us of the qualities of the Buddhas, Dharma and Sangha, thus inspiring us to develop their qualities. Some days we may feel agitated, angry or depressed. When we pass by a shrine in our homes or visit a temple and see the photos of our spiritual mentors or the peaceful figure of the Buddha, it helps us remember that there are beings who are peaceful and we can become like them. Automatically, our minds settle down.

People often like to set up a simple shrine in their homes in a clean, quiet place. Images of the Buddhas or Buddhist deities are placed on a shrine as a symbol of the Buddhas' enlightened physical forms. People following Tibetan Buddhism put photos of their spiritual teachers above these, but people from other Buddhist traditions don't necessarily do this. To the Buddha's right (the left side of the shrine as we look at it) is a text, representing the Buddha's enlightened speech. To the Buddha's left is a bell or a stupa (relic monument), symbolizing the Buddhas' enlightened mind. Various offerings are placed in front of these.

Do Buddhists worship idols?

Not at all! A piece of clay, bronze or jade is not the object of our respect and worship. When people bow before Buddha images, they recall the qualities of the enlightened beings and develop respect for their impartial love and compassion, generosity, ethical conduct, patience, joyous effort, concentration and wisdom. The statue or painting reminds people of the qualities of the Buddhas, and they bow to those qualities, not to the clay. In fact, it's not necessary to have a figure of the Buddha to bow before; we can remember the Buddhas' qualities and develop respect without it.

For example, if we go to a place far away from our family, we're likely to take a photo of them with us to remember them better. When we look at the photo and feel love for our family, we are not loving the paper and ink of the photo! The photo merely strengthens our memory. It is similar with a statue or painting of the Buddha.

Showing respect to the Buddhas and their qualities inspires us to develop these extraordinary qualities ourselves. We become like the people we respect, so when we take the loving-kindness and wisdom of the Buddhas as our example, we strive to become like them.

What is the purpose of making offerings to the Buddhas?

We don't make offerings because the Buddhas need them. When someone has purified all defilements and enjoys the bliss that comes from wisdom, he or she certainly doesn't need an apple or an incense stick to be happy! Nor do we make offerings to win the Buddhas' favor. The Buddhas developed impartial love and compassion long ago and won't be swayed by flattery and bribery the way ordinary beings are!

Making offerings helps us create positive potential or energy and develop our good qualities. At present, we have excessive attachment and miserliness. We tend to keep the biggest and best for ourselves and give the second best or something we don't want to others. But these self-centered attitudes make us always feel poor and dissatisfied no matter how much we have. We constantly fear losing what little we do have. Such attitudes make us restless, and lead us to act dishonestly to get more things or to be unkind to others to protect what we have.

One purpose of making offerings is to pacify these destructive habits of attachment and miserliness. When making an offering, it's best to do so without any feeling of loss or regret. For this reason bowls of water are often offered on the shrine. Water is readily accessible so that we can easily offer it without attachment or miserliness. By offering in this way, we habituate ourselves to the thought and action of giving. Thus, we come to feel rich when we give and take pleasure in sharing good things with others. Don't think that the Buddhas don't receive the offerings just because the flowers and fruit are still on the shrine the next day. They can receive them, enjoying the essence of the offerings, without taking them away.

Since the Buddhas, bodhisattvas (altruistic beings), and arhats (those who have attained nirvana) are the highest of all beings, it's worthwhile to make offerings to them. We usually give gifts to our friends because we like them. Here, we offer to the holy beings because we are attracted to their qualities. We shouldn't make offerings with the intention to bribe the Buddhas: "I offered you incense, now you are obliged to grant my prayers"! Rather we practice giving with a respectful and kind attitude. If we later make a request, we do so with humility.

What is offered on the shrine?

Anything we consider beautiful can be offered. Traditional offerings are water, flowers, incense, light, perfume and food, but we can offer other things as well. Water is offered each morning and removed at the end of the day. It is thrown in a clean place or sprinkled over flowers and plants. Food that is offered should be removed from the shrine before it spoils. We may eat it or give it to others, although food that has been offered on the shrine isn't generally fed to animals.

Is there a symbolic meaning to each offering?

Yes. Flowers represent the qualities of the Buddhas and bodhisattvas, incense the fragrance of pure ethics. Light symbolizes wisdom, and perfume represents confidence in the holy beings. Offering food is like offering the nourishment of meditative concentration, and music symbolizes impermanence and the empty nature of all phenomena.

While we may physically offer one flower, mentally we can imagine the entire sky filled with beautiful flowers and offer these as well. It enriches our minds to imagine lovely things and then offer them to the Buddhas and bodhisattvas. Similarly, we can offer things mentally without placing them on the shrine. For example, when we see beautiful things in showcase windows or witness the loveliness of nature, we can mentally offer these to the Buddhas. This helps us avoid attachment to these things.

Can we offer our food before eating it?

Yes. Usually we dive into a plate of food with great attachment, little mindfulness, and even less real enjoyment. Instead, we can pause before eating and imagine the food as blissful nectar that we offer to a small Buddha made of light in our heart center (chakra). The Buddha enjoys the nectar and radiates light that fills our entire body and makes us very blissful. In this way, we remain mindful of the Buddha as well as of the process of eating. We create positive potential by offering to the Buddha, and we also enjoy the food more. Before eating, some people like to recite the verses:

To the supreme teacher, the precious Buddha;
To the supreme practice, the holy precious Dharma;
To the supreme guides, the precious Sangha;
To all the objects of refuge, we make this offering.

May we and all those around us never be separated from the Triple Gem in any of our lives. May we always have the opportunity to make offerings to them. And may we continuously receive their blessings and inspiration to progress along the path.

Chapter 18

PRAYER, RITUAL AND DEDICATING POSITIVE POTENTIAL

What is the role of prayer? Can prayers be answered?

There are many kinds of prayers. Some are designed to direct and inspire our minds toward a certain quality or aim, thus creating the causes for us to attain this. An example is praying to be more tolerant and compassionate toward others. Other prayers are for specific people or situations, for example praying for a person's illness to be cured. For any prayer to be fulfilled, the prayer alone isn't sufficient: the appropriate causes must also be created. It's not just a matter of saying, "Please, Buddha, make this and that happen. I'll relax and have tea while you do the work!" For example, if we pray to be more loving and compassionate and yet make no effort to control our anger, we aren't creating the cause for that prayer to be fulfilled. The transformation of our minds comes from our own effort, but we can pray for the Buddhas' inspiration to do so.

Receiving the blessings of the Buddhas doesn't mean that something tangible comes from the Buddha and goes into us. It means that our minds are transformed through the combined effort of the teachings and guidance of the Buddhas and bodhisattvas and our own practice. "Requesting the Buddhas' blessings" has the connotation of requesting to be inspired by them, so that our minds and actions are transformed and become more beneficial.

Some Buddhist practitioners seek to be born in a pure land in their next life, because all the conditions there are conducive for Dharma practice and it's easy to develop wisdom and compassion. But we can't pray to be born in a pure land and expect the Buddhas and bodhisattvas to do all the work! We must also make effort to actualize the teachings by not selfishly clinging to worldly pleasures and by generating compassion and understanding of emptiness. Praying then has a profound effect on our minds. On the other hand, if we make no attempt to correct our harmful habits and if our minds are distracted while we pray, then there is minimal effect.

Some people pray for another's sickness to be cured, for the family finances to improve or for a deceased relative to have a good rebirth. For these things to occur the other people involved must have created the necessary causes. If they have, our prayers provide the condition for the seed of constructive actions they did in the past to ripen into that result. However, if they haven't created the causal seeds through their own positive past actions, then it's difficult for our prayers to be fulfilled. We can put fertilizer and water on the ground, but if the farmer hasn't planted the seed, nothing will grow.

When the Buddha described how cause and effect works in our mindstreams, he said that killing causes us to have short lives or much illness. Abandoning killing or saving the lives of others causes us to have a long life, free from illness. If we neglect to follow this basic advice and yet pray for a long and healthy life, we are missing the point! On the other hand, if we have abandoned killing or saved lives, then prayers can help those positive seeds to ripen.

Similarly, the Buddha said generosity is the cause of wealth. If we have been generous in a past life and now pray for our wealth to increase, then our finances could improve.

Yet, if we are very miserly now, we are creating the causes for poverty, not wealth, in the future. Being generous—helping those in need and sharing what we have—will bring desirable results sometime in the future. On the other hand, when we experience some difficulties in our life, it's helpful to ask ourselves, "What kind of action could I have done that created the cause for this result?" We can learn more about specific actions and their results from studying the Buddha's teachings. Then we can change our behavior and thus plant more seeds in our mindstreams to experience desirable results.

What is the purpose of rituals? Are they necessary?

The purpose of rituals is to help us counteract our disturbing attitudes and actions and to develop our good qualities. Rituals are a means, not an end in themselves. Because we're beginners and often find it difficult to distinguish what to practice and what to abandon on the path, prayers written by advanced practitioners give us guidelines to follow. Saying the prayers can help us tune into the meanings they express. While we read or recite them, we can simultaneously meditate and transform our minds into the mental states described in the rituals. When we do a ritual alone, we can pause to concentrate on particular points that touch us deeply.

We needn't limit our prayers to those composed by other people. As we study the Dharma and become familiar with the path to enlightenment, prayers may spontaneously arise in our minds. Events that provoke prayers may occur in our lives, and these can be very helpful in deepening our experience of the Dharma.

Some people like rituals and find them helpful for their practice. Other people find them distracting. A person may find it helpful to do more rituals at certain times and fewer at others. Everyone is unique, and there are no hard and fast rules.

What are some of the common Buddhist rituals?

Rituals found in all Buddhist traditions include turning for refuge to the Buddha, Dharma and Sangha, taking precepts to avoid harmful behavior, praising the qualities of the Three Jewels and making offerings to them, generating loving-kindness toward others, revealing our own mistakes, and rejoicing in the happiness and good qualities of others. In addition to these, each tradition has unique prayers reflecting those aspects of the path it emphasizes.

What role does chanting play in our spiritual development?

Chanting can be very beneficial if done with a proper motivation such as preparing for future lives, seeking liberation from cyclic existence, or aiming to become a Buddha to benefit others most effectively. For chanting to be effective in helping us generate positive states of mind, we must try to concentrate and reflect upon the meaning of what we chant. There isn't much benefit if we chant while our minds are distracted by thoughts of food or work or parties. A tape recorder can also chant the names of the Buddha and say prayers! But if we transform our thoughts so they correspond to what we're chanting, then chanting becomes very powerful and beneficial.

A complete spiritual practice includes more than chanting. Listening to teachings, contemplating and discussing their meaning, and integrating them into our daily life enables us to think, feel, speak and act in beneficial ways. Chanting alone can't liberate us from cyclic existence. Deep meditation is necessary to generate the wisdom realizing selflessness.

What is the difference between a prayer and a mantra? Is it necessary to chant them in a foreign language that we don't understand?

Mantras are prescribed syllables to protect the mind. We want to protect our minds from attachment, anger, ignorance, and so on. When combined with the four opponent powers (explained in the chapter on karma), mantra recitation acts powerfully to purify negative karmic imprints on our mindstreams. While reciting mantras, we can train our minds to think, feel and visualize in beneficial ways, thus building up constructive mental and emotional habits.

Mantras are recited in Sanskrit, rather than being translated into other languages, because they are the words spoken by a Buddha while in a deep state of meditation. The sound of these syllables can induce beneficial energy or vibration. While reciting a mantra, we can concentrate on the sound of the mantra, on its meaning, or on the accompanying visualizations that our spiritual mentor has taught us.

On the other hand, the great spiritual masters composed prayers to help us develop constructive attitudes. They did this because sometimes we have difficulty dffferentiating between which attitudes and actions to practice and which to abandon in our Dharma practice. Prayers express the essence of constructive mental states, and when we think about the meaning of the prayers, our minds are transformed into those attitudes. Because it's important to understand the meaning of the prayers, they can be translated from one language to another. Although chanting prayers in Asian languages can be quite lovely and inspiring, we can also do them in our own language because this facilitates our understanding.

What does the mantra *om mani padme hum* mean?

Om mani padme hum is the mantra of the Buddha of Compassion, Avalokiteshvara (*Kuan Yin, Kannon, Chen-*

resig). The entire meaning of the path to enlightenment is contained in the six syllables of this mantra. *Om* refers to the body, speech and mind of the Buddhas, that is, what we want to attain by our practice. *Mani* means jewel, and refers to all the method aspects of the path: the determination to be free from cyclic existence, compassion, generosity, ethics, patience, joyous effort and so on. *Padme* (pronounced "pay may" by the Tibetans) means lotus, and refers to the wisdom aspect of the path. By uniting both method and wisdom in a combined practice, we can purify our mindstreams of all defilements and develop all of our potentials. *Hum* (sometimes written *hung*) refers to the mind of all the Buddhas.

Recitation of *om mani padme hum* is very effective for purifying the mind and for developing compassion. It can be recited out loud or silently, and at any time. For example, if we are waiting in a queue, instead of getting impatient and angry, we can mentally recite this mantra and generate compassionate thoughts for those around us.

There is the custom of giving an oral transmission of a mantra, which means a spiritual teacher recites it and we either listen or repeat it after him or her. This transmits to us the energy of the lineage of practitioners who have used this mantra, and it makes our recitation of the mantra more powerful. However, even without receiving the oral transmission of *om mani padme hum* one may recite it and receive benefit from its calming energy.

What is merit? Isn't it selfish to do positive actions just to get merit, as if it were spiritual money?

The English word "merit" doesn't convey the Buddhist connotation. It sounds like getting gold stars in school because you did well, and that is not the meaning intended here. First of all, no one is rewarding us. When we act constructively, we leave positive imprints or seeds on our mindstreams, and when the necessary cooperative condi-tions are present, they will bear fruit. This isn't a physical seed or imprint, but an intangible one, a positive potential.

It's neither proper nor beneficial to grasp at positive po-tential as if it were spiritual money. If we do, we are likely to quarrel with other people over who can make offerings first or become jealous of others because they do more virtuous actions than we do. Such attitudes are certainly not benefi-cial! While it's good to take advantage of opportunities to create positive potential, we should do so to improve our-selves, to create the causes for happiness and to help others, and not out of attachment or jealousy.

Why must positive potential be dedicated? What should it be dedicated for?

It's important to dedicate our positive potential so it isn't destroyed by our anger or wrong views. Just as a steering wheel guides a car, dedication guides how our positive po-tential ripens. It's best to dedicate for the most extensive and noble goals. If we do so, all the smaller results will natu-rally come. If we dedicate our positive potential, however small, toward the ultimate happiness and enlightenment of all sentient beings, this automatically includes dedicating for a good rebirth and for the happiness of our relatives and friends.

Some people think, "I have so little positive potential. If I dedicate it for the happiness of everyone, then I won't have any left over for myself." This is incorrect. Dedicating our positive potential to others doesn't deprive us of its benefits. Rather, it expands the field of who will receive benefit from our actions. While dedicating our positive potential for the benefit of all beings, we can still make special prayers for the happiness of particular people who are undergoing difficul-ties at that time.

Can merit be transferred to deceased relatives or friends?

"Dedicating" positive potential (merit) rather than "transferring" it conveys the meaning better. We can't transfer merit the way we can transfer the title to a piece of property or the way I can give you my car because you don't have one. The Buddha stated that those who create the causes are the ones who experience the results. I can't create the cause and have you experience the result, because the imprint or seed of the action has been implanted on my mindstream, not yours. So if our deceased relatives and friends didn't act constructively while they were alive, we can't create good karma and then give it to them to experience.

However, our prayers and offerings on their behalf can create the circumstances necessary so that a positive action they created can bear its fruit. When a seed is planted in a field, it needs the cooperative conditions of sunshine, water and fertilizer to grow. Likewise, a seed or imprint of an action will ripen when all the cooperative conditions are present. If the deceased have done beneficial actions while they were alive, then the additional positive potential we create by making offerings or engaging in virtuous actions— reciting and reading Dharma texts, making statues of the Buddha, contemplating love and compassion for all beings and so forth—can help them. We can dedicate the positive potential from these actions for the benefit of the deceased, and this could help their own virtuous seeds to ripen.

Chapter 19

MEDITATION

What is meditation?

Nowadays people confuse meditation with many other activities. Meditation is not simply relaxing the body and mind: we can lie on the beach or take a drink if that's what we seek. Nor is it imagining being a successful person with wonderful possessions, good relationships, appreciation from others and fame. This is merely daydreaming about things that increase our attachment to transient things. Meditation is not sitting in the full vajra position, with an arrow-straight back and a holy expression on our face. Meditation is done with the mind. Even if the body is in perfect position, if our mind is running wild thinking about objects of attachment or anger, we're not meditating.

The Tibetan word for meditation is *gom*. This has the same verbal root as the word meaning to habituate or to familiarize. Meditation means habituating ourselves to positive, constructive and realistic attitudes. It is building up good habits of the mind. Meditation is used to transform our thoughts and views so that they are more compassionate and correspond to reality.

Can meditation be dangerous? Some people say you can go crazy from it. Is that true?

If we learn to meditate from an experienced teacher who

gives instruction in a reliable method, and if we follow these instructions correctly, there is no danger at all. Meditation is simply building up good habits of the mind. This we do in a gradual fashion; it's unwise to try to do an advanced practice without proper instruction, when we are beginners. However, if we practice a reliable path in a gradual fashion, we too can become Buddhas!

How do we learn to meditate? What kinds of meditation are there?

If we wish to meditate, we must first receive instruction from a qualified teacher. Some people think they can invent their own way to meditate and that they don't need to learn from a skilled teacher. This is very unwise. It's to our advantage to listen to teachings given by a reliable source like the Buddha. These teachings have been studied by scholars and practiced by skilled meditators who have attained results throughout the centuries. In this way, we can establish that a lineage of teachings and meditation practice is valid and worthy of being practiced. These days many people teach meditation and spiritual paths, but we should examine them well and not just excitedly jump into something. If the meditation practice is one taught by the Buddha and passed down by a pure lineage, we can trust it. Such a practice was not concocted according to someone's whim.

First, we listen to teachings and then deepen our understanding by thinking about them. Then, through meditation we combine what we have learned with our mindstream. For example, we hear teachings on how to develop impartial love for all beings. Next, we check up and investigate whether that is possible. We come to understand each step in the practice. Then, we build up this good habit of the mind by integrating it with our being; we try to experience the various steps leading to impartial love. That is meditation.

There are two general kinds of meditation: one is designed to develop concentration and the other to develop understanding and wisdom. Within these two broad categories, the Buddha taught a wide variety of meditation techniques and the lineages of these are extant today. A simple meditation of observing the breath can be done to calm our mind and free it from its usual chatter. This helps us to be calmer in our daily life and not to worry so much. Other meditations help us to control anger, attachment and jealousy by developing positive and realistic attitudes toward other people. There are also purification meditations that cleanse the imprints of negative actions and stop nagging feelings of guilt. In some meditations, we try to see through the fantasies we have about who we are and build up realistic self-confidence and a positive self-image. Some meditations involve contemplating a koan—a perplexing puzzle designed to break down our usual fixed conceptions. Others involve visualization and mantra recitation. Still others necessitate thinking in constructive ways in order to gain proper understanding and eventually go beyond conceptual thought. These are a few of the many types of meditation taught in Buddhism.

What are the benefits of meditation?

By building up good habits of the mind in meditation, our behavior in daily life gradually changes. Our anger decreases, we are better able to make decisions and we become less dissatisfied and restless. These results of meditation can be experienced now. But we should always try to have a broader and more encompassing motivation to meditate than just our own present happiness. If we generate the motivation to meditate in order to make preparation for future lives, or to attain liberation from the cycle of constantly recurring problems, or to reach the state of full enlightenment for the benefit of all beings, then naturally our minds will also be peaceful now. In addition, we'll be able to attain those high and noble goals.

It's very beneficial to have a regular meditation practice, even if it's only for a short time each day. It's incorrect to think, "I'm a working person. My day is so busy with career, family, and social obligations that I can't meditate. That is the job of monks and nuns." Not at all! If meditation is helpful to us, we should make time for it every day. Even if we don't want to meditate, it's important to keep some "quiet time" for ourselves each day: a time when we can sit and reflect upon what we do and why, a time when we can read a Dharma book or do some chanting. It's extremely important that we learn to like ourselves and to be happy alone. Setting aside some quiet time, preferably in the morning before the start of the day's activities, is necessary, especially in modern societies where people are so busy. We always have time to nourish our bodies; we never skip a meal because we see it's important. Likewise, we should reserve time to nourish our mind and heart as well, because they too are important. After all, it is our mind, not our body, that continues on to future lives, carrying with it the karmic imprints of our actions. Dharma practice isn't done for the Buddha's benefit, but for our own. The Dharma describes how to create the causes for happiness, and since we all want happiness, we should practice the Dharma as much as we can.

Can one develop clairvoyant powers through practicing Buddhism? Is this a worthwhile goal to pursue?

Yes, one can, but that isn't the principal goal of the practice. Some people get very excited about the prospect of having clairvoyance. "Wait until I tell my friends about this! Everyone will think I'm special and will come to ask me for advice. I'll be well known and widely respected!" What an egotistical motivation for wanting to be clairvoyant! If we still get angry and are unable to control what we say, think and do, what use is running after clairvoyance? It could even become a distraction to our practice if we get caught up in the desire to be famous. It's far more beneficial to become a kind and altruistic person.

Once a child asked me if I had clairvoyance. Could I bend a spoon through concentration? Could I stop a clock or walk through a wall? I told him no, and even if I could, what use would it be? Would that lessen the suffering in the world? In fact, the person whose spoon I ruined may suffer more! The point of our human existence isn't to build up our egos but to develop kind hearts and a sense of universal responsibility working for world peace. Loving-kindness is the real miracle!

If one has a kind heart, then developing clairvoyant powers could be beneficial for others. High practitioners don't go around advertising their clairvoyance. In fact, most of them will deny they have such abilities and will be very humble. The Buddha warned against public displays of clairvoyance unless they were necessary to benefit others. Humble people are actually more impressive than boastful ones: their serenity and respect for others shine through. People who have subdued their pride, who have loving-kindness toward others, and who are developing their wisdom are people we can trust. Such people are working for the benefit of others, not for their own prestige and welfare.

Some Buddhist traditions use visualization and mantra recitation during meditation while others discourage these. Why?

The Buddha taught a variety of techniques because different people have different inclinations. Each technique may approach a similar goal but from a different vantage point. For example, when doing the breathing meditation, emphasis is placed on developing concentration on the breath it-self. In this case, visualizing anything else would distract us from the object of meditation, which is the breath. However, another meditation technique has the visualized image of the Buddha as its object of meditation. In this case, concentration is focused on that. A purification meditation could involve, for example, visualization of the Buddha and light radiating from the Buddha into us and all the beings who we imagine seated around us. This meditation takes the natural tendency of our mind to imagine things and transforms it into the path to enlightenment. Instead of imagining a holiday with our boyfriend or girlfriend, which just incites our attachment, we imagine the serene figure of the Buddha, which inspires a balanced and peaceful state of mind.

Similarly, reciting a mantra takes the natural tendency of our mind to chatter and transforms it into the path. Rather than continuing our unending internal dialogue about what we like and what we don't, we use our inner voice to recite mantras. Mantra recitation helps us to develop concentration and can have a purifying effect on the mind.

It is better to do just one type of meditation or a variety?

This depends on the specific Buddhist tradition we follow and on the instructions of our spiritual teacher. From a Tibetan Buddhist viewpoint, it's beneficial to develop ability in several different types of meditation because many different aspects of our character need to be cultivated. Thus, we may do breathing meditation to calm the mind, loving-kindness meditation to generate compassion and altruism for others, visualization of the Buddha or a deity along with mantra recitation to purify negative karmic imprints, and analytical meditation combined with concentration to de-velop the wisdom realizing emptiness. When we have developed a general overall view of the gradual path to enlightenment, we'll understand the purpose of each meditation and where it fits in along the path. Then we can gradually develop many different abilities and sides of our character.

Part Two
WORKING WITH ANGER

WORKING WITH ANGER

Buddhism is a science of the mind, and many of those who practice it say that the Buddha was actually a great therapist who taught practical methods for dealing with disturbing attitudes and problems. Some of these methods deal with anger and are very applicable to our daily lives.

There is nothing particularly "Buddhist" about this subject. In fact, many of the Buddha's teachings are common sense, not religious doctrine. Common sense isn't the property of any religion. Rather, it brings clarity about reasonable and beneficial ways to live. No matter what our religion is, it's helpful to look at our minds and think about how we can deal with the explosive volcano called anger.

Two basic types of meditation are found in Buddhism: one aims to develop concentration, the other insight or understanding. In Tibetan Buddhism, analysis is the key to developing understanding. Using analytic meditation, we investigate whether our thoughts, feelings and perceptions are realistic or not, beneficial or not. Do they see things as they are or do they project and exaggerate qualities? Do they make us feel peaceful and act in a kind manner or are they harmful to ourselves and others? We use analytic meditation to examine our own experiences in this light. Some people say that analytic meditation is similar to cognitive therapy.

In Buddhism, there is no word for "emotion." Rather, we speak of mental events. Some of these mental events or mental factors perceive things inaccurately and make the mind agitated. Some, like impartial love and compassion, are realistic and beneficial. The essence of spiritual practice involves uprooting the former and cultivating the latter. We can do this because, according to Buddhism, there is no fixed, solid personality. What we call "I" or "me" is a combination of our body and various types of consciousness and mental events, and all of these are in a constant state of change.

Buddhism doesn't make the same distinction between thinking and feeling that we make in the West. In the West, we believe that thought is conceptual and emotions aren't. But according to Buddhism, anger, for example, is conceptual. When someone points out our mistake, for instance, we may think, "Everyone always criticizes me unjustly." That thought is distorted, for everyone doesn't always criticize us unjustly. But because of it, we are unable to bear what the other person said and may wish to harm that person in return.

That angry mental state can strongly motivate our physical and verbal actions. Anger is also related to the body—to the energy in our body as well as to hormones such as adrenaline, which influence our body. However, anger itself is not an aroused state of the body: it is an emotion in our mind. Some people may first recognize physical indications of anger, such as muscle tension, and then know they are feeling angry. However, when we develop mindfulness, we'll be able to detect that anger first arises in the mind, and the physical symptoms follow afterward.

Is Anger Realistic or Beneficial?

Before examining whether anger is realistic or beneficial let's define it. From the Buddhist perspective, anger is an attitude that exaggerates the negative qualities of a person, situation or thing, or superimposes negative qualities that aren't there, and then rejects or wants to harm the person or object. The word *anger* as it's used here is a generic term for any kind of aversion and includes being annoyed, irritated, critical, judgmental, self-righteous, belligerent and hostile. Just by the definition, we can see that anger is unrealistic: it exaggerates or superimposes negative qualities. For example, a person who insults us may have many good qualities, but we disregard these and focus on one fault, going over and over it in our minds, feeling more and more that it is unbearable. Anger perceives a situation not in a balanced way, but through a distorted filter. By reflecting on our own experiences, we can see that when we're angry, we're viewing a situation through the filter of "me, I, my and mine." We think that the way the situation appears to us is how it really exists out there, objectively; but we're actually viewing it through the veil of our own self-centeredness. It's clear that if we look at the same situation from another person's perspective, it appears differently. So how can our anger be a correct, objective interpretation?

Is anger beneficial? If we take an honest look at our own experiences, we have to admit that anger has many disadvantages. When we're angry, we're unhappy. Making mountains out of molehills, we get caught up in a flurry of irritation. Anger makes us lose control of ourselves, so we speak cruelly to others and even physically harm those we love. We say and do things that we regret later. Thus, anger often leads to feelings of remorse and guilt. Who among us doesn't have a hidden cache of events that we don't like to remember because we're ashamed of how we acted on those occasions?

Sometimes we wonder why others avoid us—after all, we think we're pretty nice people! But if we examine how we've treated others, especially when we've been angry, then it's clear how our relationships have been damaged. Let's think back to a situation when we were angry. Now, let's step out of our own shoes and look at ourselves from the other person's view. How do our actions and words appear from the other's viewpoint? Did we act in a kind manner? Would we have wanted to be our own friend at that time?

In 1989, an incredulous journalist asked His Holiness the Dalai Lama, "After the massive destruction the Chinese communist government has wreaked on your country and people, why aren't you angry? How can you tell the Tibetan people to have compassion for their oppressors?" His Holiness responded, "What good would it do to be angry? If I got angry, then I wouldn't be able to sleep at night or eat my meals peacefully. I'd get ulcers and my health would deteriorate. My anger couldn't change the past or improve the future, so what use would it be? However, with compassion we Tibetans can act to improve the situation."

The Buddha never said, "You shouldn't feel anger. You're bad and sinful if you get angry." There's no judgment involved. When we're angry, our anger simply exists at that moment. We shouldn't ignore it. However, to make peace with our past and with other people we must grow beyond anger and let go of it.

When examining the defects of anger, it's important not to get mad at or blame ourselves because we get angry. That only compounds the problem. There's no need to beat up on ourselves emotionally. The fact that we got angry doesn't mean we're bad people, it just means that we temporarily let a harmful emotion overrun us. We're not yet well trained in patience, but we can gradually develop this quality. It's helpful to remember that we are not our anger: anger is a thought or feeling that may produce certain physiological states, and all of these are temporary.

An Alternative to Expressing or Repressing Anger

Some people say that anger is a natural and automatic emotion which we all experience in reaction to harm. The issue is if, when and how to express it in a healthy way. Buddhism goes a step further and asks, "Must anger be a foregone conclusion in reaction to harm? Is it desirable and possible to eliminate anger from the root so that it isn't there at all?" Many of the people we admire—the Buddha, Jesus, Mahatma Gandhi and others—had the ability to remain internally undisturbed in the face of harm and yet externally act for the benefit of others. Their anger was neither repressed nor expressed; it was simply absent, having been transformed into tolerance and compassion.

In other words, there is an alternative to either expressing or repressing anger. According to Buddhism, if we repress anger, our emotions are still unresolved, and this could be physically or mentally damaging to ourselves. If we act out our anger, we establish the habit to feel and act on anger again in the future. In addition, what we say or do could easily hurt others. Expressing anger is one extreme and repressing it is another. In both cases, the trace of anger remains in one form or another.

Patience is an alternative. It is the ability to remain internally calm and undisturbed in the face of harm or difficulties. It's a mental attitude, which is very different from pasting a plastic smile on our faces while hatred simmers inside. Patience means dissolving the anger energy so that it's no longer there. Then, with a clear mind, we can evaluate various alternatives and decide what to say and do to remedy the situation. It's important to differentiate mental attitudes from external actions. We can be angry inside and act in either a passive or aggressive manner. Or we can be patient internally, and externally either let things blow over or be assertive. Patience gives us the mental space to choose how to act and then to act appropriately.

Sometimes we may have to speak strongly to others because that is the only way to communicate with them. For example, if your child is playing in the street and you very sweetly say, "Susie dear, please don't play in the street," she may ignore you. On the other hand, if you speak forcefully and explain the danger to her, she'll remember and obey. But your mind can be calm—not angry—when you do this. And your child will sense the difference between the same words said when you're centered versus when you're upset.

Doubts

Some people doubt the validity of letting go of or transforming anger. Some say anger is a source of information, or it's an antidote to vulnerability, guilt, self-blame and repression, for example in the case of abuse. Others believe that anger helps us win when we play sports. Some say anger is good because it motivates us to correct social injustice or to stop harmful situations. Some people are concerned that forgiving others' harmful behavior is tantamount to condoning it.

Some say anger can be a source of information that other people's behavior is not acceptable. But in examining any particular situation, we must determine whether the behavior is unacceptable according to basic societal and ethical standards of human decency or unacceptable to our own selfish concern that wants all its desires fulfilled. There's a big difference between the two. In the former, people may transgress basic ethical values, and although presently anger may arise in response, we must still question, "Is it the only possible response that can let us know people have crossed boundaries they shouldn't?" Couldn't a clear and calm mind also discern this? Also, is anger the only emotion that will give us the energy to counteract the harm? Again, there are alternate responses, such as compassion, that can motivate us to act.

Anger is a source of information in that it lets us know that our mind is disturbed and that our buttons are being pushed. But rather than acting according to our habitual pattern of blaming others for our anger, we can start to ask ourselves, "What buttons are being pushed? Can I do something about my buttons?" Our buttons getting pushed depends on two things: us having the buttons and another person's actions. If we remove our buttons, there won't be anything for others to push! Of course, doing this requires a lot of internal work on our part.

Protection from Vulnerability or Guilt?

Is anger a good antidote to feelings of vulnerability, guilt and self-blame, for example in cases of child abuse, rape or divorce? Some people feel vulnerable if they let go of their protective shields of anger. Fears abound: "My anger is justified. I don't want it to go away because then what will happen to me? Who will I be? How can I feel self-dignity without being outraged at what others have done to me?" It's helpful to explore further and recognize that anger arises due to pain and fear. These emotions must also be acknowledged and accepted, but they too are mental events—temporary feelings that arise in our minds but that aren't us. In Buddhism, we practice observing the arising, abiding and disappearing of these mental factors without the knee-jerk reactions of either rejecting the feelings or letting them overwhelm us. Whether we reject a feeling or become attached to it, the result is similar—that emotion controls us. When we can allow an emotion to be without either pushing it away or buying into its storyline, it will gradually lose its power over us because we cease feeding into it. Feelings dissipate by themselves because they are transient by their very nature.

In therapy, it may be necessary to express anger in a safe situation with the therapist as a way to acknowledge its presence. Buddhism says that we can't do anything about our anger unless we first acknowledge it and know it's there. However, I don't believe that continually releasing anger through shouting in an empty field or beating pillows is helpful in the long run. It could reinforce the mental habit of anger as well as encourage its expression physically. What happens if sometime clients get angry and there aren't any pillows around to beat or they aren't in a place where they can shout and not bother others? They may then act out their anger on whatever or whomever is around, causing more problems to themselves and others.

When we're angry, it's harmful to judge ourselves, thinking we're bad because we're angry. The anger is just what is at that moment; it's what's happening. After acknowledging the existence of anger, we can go on to question, "Do we want to continue to be angry? Does anger help us? Is it realistic?" Based on what was explained earlier, no. If we are to heal, we have to go beyond anger.

Some people get stuck in their anger. It does give us a buzz, a surge of energy and a sense of power. But it also makes us unhappy. And because it clouds our minds, it prevents us from communicating well with others. So, expressing anger isn't an end in itself: we must apply antidotes to anger to dissolve it so that it no longer exists. Some antidotes will be explained in a moment.

Anger and Sports

To address the concern of the sports enthusiast: yes, anger may help us win the game, but is that beneficial? Is it worthwhile to reinforce a negative characteristic just to get a trophy? Our minds become very tight when we make "us versus them" too concrete: "*My* team must win. We have to fight and beat the enemy."

But let's step back for a moment. Why do we want to win and want the other team to lose? The only reason is because we think, "My team is best because it's mine." Of course the other team feels the same way. Who is right? Competition based on such self-centeredness isn't productive because it breeds anger and jealousy.

On the other hand, we can concentrate on the process of

playing the game, rather than on the goal of winning. In this case, we'll enjoy the physical exercise, the camaraderie and team spirit, whether we win or lose. Psychologically, this attitude will bring more happiness. Competitive sports may be a societally accepted way of venting anger, but they don't cure the anger. They only temporarily release the physical energy accompanying anger. We're still avoiding the real problem: our misconceptions of people and situations.

Outrage at Social Injustice

Another doubt concerns the idea that anger is good because it energizes us to act to correct social injustice or to stop harm from occurring. But is anger the only motivation that can energize us to correct harmful situations? According to Buddhism, no. Compassion—the wish for others to be free from problems and confusion—is not only a powerful motivator but also one that is more balanced, realistic and effective than anger. Although we may initially react in anger to injustice, by applying the techniques described below, we can transform our attitude to a more compassionate one before acting.

The difficulty with accepting anger as a motivator to remedy social injustice is that our minds become exactly like the minds of those we oppose. Both are angry, both consider their position right and the other's wrong. Both have a hard time listening to the needs and interests of the other party. Both think the other should change. We know what usually happens when we approach conflict situations with such attitudes. Self-righteous indignation doesn't lead to communication, cooperation or compromise.

In the West, we sometimes confuse compassion with passivity, icky-gooey sentimentality or Pollyanna idealism. From the Buddhist perspective, it's none of these. Compassion is an attitude which realizes that others' wish to be happy and to avoid difficulties is just as intense and worthy of respect as our own. Others may be confused and use harmful methods in their endeavor to be happy. That has to be remedied. But their wish for happiness is to be honored. If we can see that both the victim and the perpetrator of harm equally want to be happy and free from suffering, we can intervene to stop harmful situations with compassion for both sides, not compassion for just the victim and vengefulness for the perpetrator. Perpetrators act as they do because they aren't happy. Compassion wishes them to be happy, to be free from the tortured states of mind or the frustrating situations that lead them to violence. We can feel compassion toward these people and at the same time forcefully intervene to stop them from harming others.

Forgiving

Sometimes we feel that if we forgive the people who harmed us it's tantamount to condoning their harmful behavior. This isn't the case at all. We can recognize that a certain behavior was harmful and shouldn't be continued in the future, and at the same time we can let go of our anger toward the person who did it. There are two things to consider here: first, the behavior and the person who did it are separate. We can say the behavior or the intention motivating it were harmful, but we can't say that the person is evil. From a Buddhist perspective, each being has the innate potential to become a fully enlightened Buddha. Each person has some internal goodness that can never be destroyed, no matter how badly he or she may act. Recognizing this, we can forgive others because they make mistakes just as we do, and we can simultaneously say that a particular action is harmful or unacceptable.

Second, forgiving benefits ourselves. When we hold onto our anger, we're tense and unhappy, and this can affect our relationships and physical health. Therefore, it's to our own advantage to seek to practice patience and let go of our resentment.

Of course we can't force ourselves to dissolve the anger or to forgive someone. Sometimes we first may need to remove ourselves physically from the stress-provoking person or situation to get some mental distance. Then, through practicing the antidotes to anger, we can gradually dissolve it. At this point the spaciousness, clarity and gentleness of forgiveness will naturally arise in our hearts.

It's important to remember that forgiving others doesn't mean we tolerate damaging behavior or return to a harmful situation. Nor does it necessitate sharing our forgiveness with the other people if they could misconstrue it and resume their harmful behavior.

Training in Patience

What can we do when we're angry? The Buddha described a variety of techniques for developing patience. Many of these are found in *A Guide to the Bodhisattva's Way of Life*, by the great Indian sage Shantideva.

The general strategy is as follows: first, we need to learn the techniques for dealing with anger. Then we can begin to practice them in our meditation sessions. This builds up our familiarity with and confidence in these new ways of thinking. By practicing these techniques while seated on our meditation cushion in a peaceful environment, we'll build up a repertoire of alternative ways to look at situations that used to make us angry.

Training ourselves in these techniques when we're not angry is important. It's like learning to drive. We don't go on the highway during rush hour the first day behind the wheel because we're not yet prepared for the challenges it presents. Instead, we drive around a parking lot to familiarize ourselves with the accelerator, the brakes and the steering wheel. By first practicing in a safe environment, we'll be able to handle the car in more difficult situations later on.

Similarly, we need to start practicing patience when we're not in a conflict situation. We can do this while we sit quietly by remembering previous situations in which we exploded in anger, or events that even now make us hostile or hurt when we think about them. Then we apply the techniques to those: we rerun a mental video of an event, only we try to think differently in it. By viewing the situation from a new perspective, our anger will decrease, and we can then envision ourselves responding to the other people differently.

This kind of practice not only helps us dissolve past hurt and grudges, it also makes us familiar with techniques that we can apply in similar situations in the future. Then when a situation occurs in our lives and we feel our anger arising, we can select a technique and use it.

Sometimes it's hard to dissolve our anger even when we're in a peaceful environment, because we've become locked into our past emotions and misconceptions. But if we keep on trying, we'll gradually learn to subdue them. Then, when we go to work, school or family gatherings, we'll have at least a "fighting chance" to work with our anger should it arise. With constant practice over time, we'll be able to prevent anger from arising at all.

Subduing anger is a slow and steady process. Don't expect it to disappear overnight. Reacting in anger is a deeply ingrained habit, and like all bad habits, it takes time to unlearn. Developing patience requires a great deal of effort— and patience!

Recognizing We're Angry

Before we can eliminate or transform our anger, we must first be able to identify it. Sometimes we have difficulty recognizing that we're feeling annoyed, irritated, hostile or belligerent. This happens because often we are distracted by the external environment and thus become out of touch with our own feelings. Or, we may know something is the matter, but not know what it is. There are several ways to investigate and identify our feelings. For example, we can observe what distractions arise when we are trying to focus on the inhalation and exhalation of the breath during meditation on the breath. We may recognize a general feeling of restlessness or anger. Or we may remember a situation from years ago that we're still irritated about. By noting these distractions, we'll know what we need to work on.

Another way to identify our anger is by becoming aware of our physical reactions. For example, if we feel our stomach tighten, our jaws clench or our body temperature increase, it could be a signal that we're starting to become angry. Each person has different physical manifestations of anger. We can observe and note what ours are. This is helpful, for sometimes it's easier to identify the physical sensations accompanying anger than the anger itself.

Another way is to observe our moods. When we're in a bad mood, we can pause and ask ourselves, "What is this feeling? What has happened to prompt it?" Sometimes we can observe patterns in our moods and behaviors. This gives us clues as to how our minds operate, and what our anger clings to.

Dealing with Criticism

Here are some examples of difficult situations and various antidotes to use for working with anger. Receiving criticism frequently prompts our anger, and it seems as if all of us get criticized more often than we'd like. We have to work so hard to get some things—like money—but criticism comes without our even needing to ask for it!

When we're criticized we usually feel we're the only person that gets dumped on, don't we? "I'm doing my best, but the boss always overlooks others' mistakes and inevitably notices mine. Everybody's always getting on my case!" Interestingly, when we talk to other people, we notice that almost everyone feels he or she is criticized unfairly or too much. It's not just us. Actually, our problems appear bigger than those of others because we're self-absorbed.

When someone criticizes us, our instant reaction is anger. What is prompting this response? Our conception of the situation. Although we may not be consciously aware of it, one part of our mind holds the view, "I'm a great person. If I slip up and make a mistake, it's a small one. This person has completely misunderstood the situation. He's making a big deal out of my little mistake and declaring it at the top of his voice to the whole world! He's wrong!" This description is oversimplified, but if we're honest with ourselves, we may recognize that this is what we think and feel. But are these conceptions correct? Are we perfect or nearly so? Obviously not.

Take a situation in which we make a mistake and someone notices it. If that person were to come along and tell us we have a nose on our face, would we be angry? No. Why not? Because it's obvious that we have a nose. It's there for the world to see. Someone merely saw it and commented upon it. It's the same with our mistakes and faults. They're there, they're obvious, and the world sees them. That person is merely commenting on what is evident to him and others. Why should we get angry? If we aren't upset when someone says we have a nose, why should we be when he tells us we have faults?

We'd be more relaxed if we acknowledged, "Yes, you're right. I made a mistake." Or, "Yes. I have a bad habit." Instead of putting on the act of "I'm perfect. How dare you say that!" we could just admit our error and apologize. Saying "I'm sorry" frequently diffuses the situation.

It's so hard for us to say "I'm sorry," isn't it? We feel we're losing something by apologizing, we're becoming less, we're not worthwhile. We fear the other person will have power over us if we admit our mistake. Such fear makes us defensive. However, all of these are our projections. Being able to apologize indicates our inner strength. We have enough strength, honesty and self-confidence that we don't have to pretend to be faultless. We can admit our mistakes. Having faults doesn't make us a basket case! So many tense situations can be diffused by the simple words, "I'm sorry." Often all the other person wants is for us to acknowledge his or her pain and our role in it.

Similarly, when others apologize to us, it's important to accept it. If we continue to hold a grudge after someone has apologized to us, we only torment ourselves, and if we retaliate, we harm them. What use is either of these? Vengefully inflicting misery on others can't undo the past. This doesn't mean that accepting another's apology will instantly free us from all of the ramifications of his or her behavior. However, it can release us from the tension of bitterness and hostility. When we find it difficult to accept another's apology, it's wise to reflect again on some of the techniques to transform hurt and anger.

Also, if we've considered others' criticisms and they are true, then these people are in fact helping us to improve. We often say, "I want to improve. I want to eliminate my weaknesses and become a kinder person." Yet, when people tell us how to do this—especially if it is with a loud or biting tone of voice—we don't want to hear! We cry, "Hold on! You can tell me how to improve only when I want to hear it, only with a kind attitude and pleasant voice, and only if I can handle it at this moment." Wow! That's a lot to expect of other people! Since we can't control when, what, why and how others give us negative feedback, we may have to strengthen our own abilities to process it constructively. This can be done by concentrating on the relevant content of what they said and using it to improve ourselves. If we do this, then we'll be able to thank others sincerely for their comments, no matter how they have expressed them. In fact, excellent practitioners even seek out criticism!

Let's change the situation slightly. This time, suppose we're criticized for something we didn't do. Or, we made a small mistake and the other person accuses us of a huge one. Still, there's no reason to get angry. This is like somebody telling us we have horns on our head. We don't have horns. The person who says that is mistaken. Similarly, if someone blames us unjustly, there's no reason to become angry or depressed because what he or she says is incorrect.

Of course this doesn't mean we should passively accept someone's incorrect speech without attempting to rectify the misunderstanding. We need to use our discriminating wisdom to examine each situation individually. Sometimes it's better just to let it go, and not try to correct it, even later. If it's a trivial matter, the other person may later realize the mistake. Even if she doesn't, it may only start a bigger argument if we tried to explain what happened. For example, if our roommate is in a bad mood and picks at us over something small, it may be better to let it go. Because he or she is already irritable, if we try to explain at that time, the person may get even angrier. And we would be nagging the other person for nagging us! Similarly, it would be a nuisance to correct everyone every time he or she says anything inaccurate. Besides, no one would like having us around!

In other situations, we need to explain our actions and the evolution of the misunderstanding to the other person even though it is painful. It's our responsibility to do that, and to do our best to assuage their anger. However, it's best to discuss such misunderstandings or disagreements when neither we nor the other person are in the heat of anger. For one thing, we don't express ourselves well when we're angry, and this makes the situation worse. If someone shouts at us, we generally find it difficult to listen to what he says simply because his way of saying it is so disagreeable. So first we need to calm down, ideally by practicing some of the techniques for pacifying anger. Similarly, if we speak angrily to others, they won't listen to us. Thus, we need to let the other person calm down and approach him later when his mind is more open.

When we explain our actions and the evolution of the misunderstanding to the other person, it's more effective to speak gently, rather than antagonistically. We don't lose anything by being humble and offering an honest explanation. It's cruel and arrogant to dismiss another's feeling by saying, "Your anger is your problem" or to ignore someone we've quarreled with.

There may be other situations in which no overt disagreement has occurred yet we are uncomfortable with or inconvenienced by another person's actions. It's natural for such events to arise simply because we share an environment and resources. We need to communicate with others and perhaps give them negative feedback. But for it to be truly effective, we must do this with a motivation of kindness, not anger. Although we may angrily explode and this may wake the others up and inspire discussion, it may also make the situation worse or prevent communication. Thus it's best if we can first use one of the techniques described here to subdue our own hostility and then approach the others involved, explain to them how the situation appears in our eyes, how we feel about it and why, without blaming them for our feelings. We can share with them our interests and concerns and listen to theirs and try to come up with a solution that benefits all parties as much as possible.

Sometimes finding a satisfactory resolution is difficult. A person once asked His Holiness the Dalai Lama, "Someone at my office often is verbally abusive. I've tried to practice patience, and I've also tried to discuss the situation with the person. But my anger remains and the situation is too stressful for me. What should I do?" His Holiness responded, "If you feel the situation is more than you can handle right now, you could change jobs!"

When Our Religion Is Criticized

We may wonder, "What do we do when people criticize our religious beliefs?" What they think is their opinion, and they're entitled to have it. Of course, we don't necessarily agree with it. Sometimes we can give others information and correct their misconceptions, but sometimes people are closed-minded and find it difficult to listen to other views. There's nothing we can do then except maintain our kind attitude toward them.

Others' criticism cannot hurt the Dharma or the Buddha. The path to enlightenment exists whether others recognize it as such or not. We don't need to be defensive. In fact, if we become agitated when others criticize Buddhism, it indicates we're attached to our beliefs—our ego is involved and so we feel compelled to prove our beliefs are right. But we don't need others' approval to practice the Dharma. If we've examined the Buddha's teachings well and are thus secure in what we believe, others' criticism won't disturb our peace of mind. Why should it? Criticism doesn't mean our beliefs are wrong, nor does it mean we're stupid or bad. It's simply another's opinion, that's all.

Acting or Relaxing

Another technique for working with anger is quite simple. Let's say we're in a terrible situation. If we can remedy it, why get angry? We can act, we can change it. On the other hand, if we can't alter the situation, why get angry? There's nothing we can do, so we're better off accepting the situation and relaxing. Getting agitated only compounds the suffering that's already there.

This technique is also good for people who worry a lot.

Ask yourself, "Can I do something about this situation?" If the answer is yes, then there's no need to worry. Act. If the answer is no, worry is again useless. Relax and accept the situation.

How Our Energy Gets Us into Difficult Situations

Another technique to counteract anger is to examine how we became involved in the situation. Often we feel we're the innocent victim of unfair people or circumstances. "Poor me! I'm innocent. I didn't do anything and now this nasty person is taking advantage of me!"

That's a victim mentality, isn't it? By getting angry, we make ourselves the victim. Other people don't make us victims. We may be the object of another's anger or abuse, but we needn't be the victim of it. Someone else may blame or harm us, but we become a victim and become trapped in a victim mentality only when we conceive of the situation in a certain way and get angry. The meaning of this is quite profound. Let's look at it in more depth, first using an example of two adults in conflict.

Suppose our partner is upset with our behavior and lashes out at us. We often react by feeling, "Poor me. I didn't do anything but I'm getting dumped on unfairly." Is this interpretation of our experience accurate? Instead of immediately losing our temper and blaming the other person, let's recognize that this situation arose in dependence on many factors. It depends on the other person, and it also depends on us.

First, let's look at what we did in this life that has resulted in our being mistreated. How did we get into this situation? Did we do something that aggravated or hurt the other person and made him act this way toward us? Looking inside, we must be honest with ourselves. Maybe we really weren't so innocent. Maybe we were trying to manipulate the other person and he didn't fall for it. He got upset and then we acted hurt and offended. But in fact, our own behavior contributed to the situation.

Some people may be concerned that this is blaming the victim and encouraging people to take responsibility for others' behavior. It isn't. For example, a woman may have done something innocently or intentionally that annoyed her husband, but it isn't her fault if he beats her. Nor is his behavior acceptable. However, if she can look at the situation from a wide perspective, she may notice that in some instances, her unclear behaviors trigger his. This will give her the power to avoid those behaviors. Or, she may recognize that her own emotional attachments keep her in a harmful situation. This gives her the power to counteract them and free herself from an unproductive relationship.

By being introspective, we can notice our shortcomings and then try to correct them. Doing this will help us avoid finding ourselves in similar unpleasant situations in the future. We can also take whatever responsibility is ours for being in a situation, regardless of whether or not the other person is acting fairly. By acknowledging our mistakes or misdirected motivations, we'll become aware of how our behavior affects other people. By avoiding destructive behavior in the future, we won't set the stage for others to harm us.

Examining the role our own behavior played in the evolution of a bad situation doesn't mean blaming ourselves for things that aren't our responsibility and feeling guilty as a result. Getting down on ourselves is actually another trick of the self-centered attitude. It exaggerates our own importance by thinking, "If I'm not the best, then at least I'll be the worst."

We generally frame unfortunate or painful circumstances in terms of blame. Either one party or the other is to blame. "Fault" and "blame" are very harsh words in our culture: they imply being evil and guilty, and this way of conceiving situations leads to a dead end. If the ot her is to blame, then we become angry, outraged and vindictive. If we are to blame, then we become depressed and self-destructive. It's impossible to heal when we're caught up in blaming. But why do we need to frame the situation in terms of blame at all? Every situation arises from many causes and conditions. We can observe the ones we've contributed and try to abstain from them in the future. We can notice the ones others have contributed, and even though we don't condone their actions, we can feel compassion for their confusion.

For example, we want to spend more time with a friend, but he or she is preoccupied with other affairs. Feeling ignored, we grumble about it. That irritates our friend who then avoids us. In this case, we needn't blame ourselves for complaining or blame our friend for being insensitive. Instead, we can realize that the situation is dependently arising: some of the causes came from me, some from my friend. Both of us were reacting in habitual patterns rather than recognizing what we were feeling and trying to communicate it in a kind and accurate way to the other. Recognizing this, we can have compassion for both parties, and after coming to some clarity about our own feelings, we can discuss the situation with our friend.

We can also look at unfortunate events from a broader viewpoint—in the light of many lifetimes. This involves the topic of karma or intentional actions. As was discussed earlier, our physical, verbal and mental actions leave imprints on our consciousness. These imprints later will ripen and influence our experiences. What we are experiencing now is a result of thoughts, feelings, words and deeds in previous lifetimes. Let's say someone beats us. To experience that effect now, we must have done something previously, in this case, physically harmed others. Karma—action and its result—is like a boomerang. We throw it out and it comes back to us. Similarly, if we treat others in a certain way, we put that energy out and something similar will come back to us later.

Understanding this allows us to accept some responsibility for the situation. We're not a victim. We've harmed many others in the past—even in this life we can see that we've sometimes caused harm. As children we fought with other kids on the playground; as adults we've hurt others' feelings.

When we're confronted by difficult situations, it's helpful to remember that we're experiencing the long-term results of these actions. It's not surprising: the imprints of our own negative actions are ripening. If we acknowledge this, we'll see there's no reason to be hostile toward others. They are just the cooperative condition. We created the principal cause for our being in this situation ourselves.

However, we shouldn't misinterpret this and masochistically blame ourselves for everything: "I'm so awful. I deserve to have everyone persecute and take advantage of me." Such a view is totally incorrect. Instead, we acknowledge, "Yes, I harmed others in the past. Now the result is coming back to me. This doesn't mean I'm a bad person, it simply means that under the influence of my own anger or attachment, I acted mistakenly and harmed others in the past. If I don't like this experience, then I'd better be careful how I act toward other people in the future. If I don't like people to shout at me, I should be aware of how I speak to others so that I don't again create the causes to meet with similar painful situations in the future."

In this way, we'll learn from our mistakes. It isn't important to remember the exact action we did in a past life that brought about our present problem. It's sufficient to have a general feeling for the kinds of actions we could have done in the past that precipitated the present occurrence. Then we can make a strong determination not to do those actions in the future. A small book entitled *The Wheel of Sharp Weapons* by Dharmaraksita explains the links between our current experiences and our past actions. It also encourages us to abandon the self-centered attitude that spurs us to act negatively.

By training ourselves to think in this way, we can transform bad situations into the path to enlightenment. How? We think about them in constructive ways; we cease framing situations in terms of blame, fault and guilt; we examine how we came to be in difficulty and what we can do to alter it; we learn from our experiences rather than get stuck in a victim mentality.

How the Enemy Benefits Us

For the sake of simplicity, we'll use the term "enemy" to describe anyone whom we don't get along with at a particular moment. Thus even people whom we deeply care about can, at times, become our enemies when they do things that seem contrary to our interests, happiness or welfare. We often see people who go back and forth between being friends and enemies, depending upon how they're interacting at the time.

It may initially seem like a contradiction, but we can regard our enemies as friends who benefit us. First, by harming us they make our negative karma ripen, so that specific karma is now finished. Second, by harming us, they force us to examine our actions and decide how we want to act in the future. Thus, people who harm us are helping us to grow. They're kinder to us than our friends who don't offer us such challenges!

In fact, enemies are kinder to us than the Buddha. This may sound almost inconceivable: "What do you mean my enemy is kinder to me than the Buddha? The Buddha has perfect compassion for everyone. The Buddha doesn't harm a fly! How can my enemy who is such a jerk be kinder than the Buddha?"

We can look at it this way: to become Buddhas, we need to practice patience and become more tolerant. This is an essential practice: there's no way to become a Buddha without developing this quality. Have you ever heard of an irritable or intolerant Buddha? But whom can we practice patience with? Not with the Buddhas, because they don't make us angry. Not with our friends, because they're nice to us. Who gives us the opportunity to practice patience? Who is so kind and helps us develop that infinitely good quality of patience? Only the person who harm us. Only our enemy. That is why our enemies are much kinder to us than the Buddha.

My teacher made this very clear to me. At one time, I was the vice-director of a group. The director, Sam, and I didn't get along at all. During the day, I would get very mad at him, and in the evening I'd go back to my room and think, "I blew it again. What does Shantideva suggest in *A Guide to the Bodhisattva's Way of Life?*" Finally, I left that job and went to Nepal where I saw my teacher, Zopa Rinpoche. We were sitting on the roof of his house, looking at the Himalayas, so peaceful and calm. Then Rinpoche asked me, "Who's kinder to you, Sam or the Buddha?"

I thought, "You've got to be kidding! There's no comparison. The Buddha is obviously so kind, but Sam is another case!" So I replied, "The Buddha, of course."

Rinpoche looked at me as if to say, "Wow! You still haven't gotten the point!" and said, "Sam gave you the opportunity to practice patience. The Buddha didn't. You can't practice patience with the Buddha. Therefore, Sam is kinder to you than the Buddha."

I sat there dumbfounded, trying to digest what Rinpoche said. Slowly, as the years have gone by, it has sunk in. It's interesting to see yourself change when you let yourself think in this way. Now when I see Sam I appreciate what I learned from him and regret that at the time I wasn't able to completely benefit from working with him.

Thus, focusing on the benefit received from the enemy is another way to work with our anger and practice patience. We can take a bad situation as a challenge to help us grow.

Giving the Pain to the Self-Cherishing Thought

Still another technique is to give the harm and the pain to our self-cherishing thought, which is our real enemy. Our society has an interesting, and contradictory, attitude about selfishness. On one hand, our culture is very individualistic and we're taught from childhood to compete with others, to be better than them, to win, to acclaim our qualities, not to let anyone else push us around or take advantage of us. On the other hand, we're taught not to be selfish because it's impolite and others won't like us—or at least, if we're going to be selfish, do it discreetly so that others don't know.

Most people in our society view someone like Saddam Hussein as a madman—someone whose self-centered goals destroyed the happiness of even his own countrypeople. From his own perspective, however, he thought he was right and believed his actions to be beneficial. But many people think, "Clearly, he was wrong! How could he possibly think he was right?" But it's interesting, isn't it, that when we do something that others object to, we're not being self-centered—it's just that we're right and they're obviously wrong!

As we become more aware of our thoughts and actions and how they influence us and others, we'll begin to notice that our self-centeredness causes many problems. Self-centeredness propels us to say and do things that hurt others, things we're later ashamed of. Almost every conflict we have with others involves selfishness: we want our way, other people want theirs. We're convinced our idea is right, they're convinced theirs is. In addition, the selfish attitude is one of the biggest obstacles to gaining spiritual realizations because it causes us to be lazy in our Dharma practice. Thus, the real enemy that obstructs our happiness and well-being is the self-cherishing attitude, but it will us take some time thinking about this to become firmly convinced of it.

When people criticize, betray or attack us, we're hurt and angry. We feel, "How dare they treat me like this!" That attitude views the event only from our own perspective. We're preoccupied with *me, my* feelings, what is happening to *me.* Much of our emotional pain in this situation comes from our self-centeredness. However, this attitude isn't inherently us. It's like a thief in a house, and we can kick it out once we recognize it's dangerous. From a Buddhist perspective, it's possible to separate the person from his or her attitude of unhealthy self-preoccupation.

Once we become convinced that self-centeredness is neither beneficial nor an inseparable part of us, we can take any pain we experience and give it to the selfish attitude. Instead of feeling, "This is awful. I don't like listening to what this person is saying," we can think, "Great! All this pain and uncomfortable feeling I'll give to my selfish attitude. It's the real enemy, so let it take the blame." Then we can chuckle, "Ha, ha, selfish attitude. Instead of letting you make me unhappy, I'll give you this pain and worry!" This techniques is not to be confused with blaming ourselves or assuming responsibility for things that aren't our doing. Here, we are differentiating between ourselves and the real troublemaker, our self-centered attitude. Then, because we want ourselves to be happy, we give the trouble to the self-centeredness.

If we do this practice properly and sincerely, then when someone criticizes or harms us, we'll be happy, not because we're masochistic, but because we've given the damage to the real enemy, our self-centeredness. Thus we are no longer upset, and in addition, because our enemy—the selfish attitude—is suffering, we'll rejoice. Then, the more someone harms us, the happier we'll be! In fact, we'll think, "Come on, criticize me some more. I want my self-cherishing attitude to be harmed." This is a profound thought training technique. The first time I heard it, I thought, "This is impossible! What do you mean I'm supposed to be happy when someone criticizes me? How can I possibly practice this?"

But one time I did practice it, and it was remarkable! I was on pilgrimage in Asia, travelling on horseback to a remote site. One day, something was wrong with the horse my companion Henry was riding, so he had to walk and lead the horse by the reins. Henry was hungry and tired from the long journey. On top of that, he had to walk instead of ride. Since I felt okay, I offered him my horse.

I don't understand why, but this upset Henry. And, as often happens when people get angry, they remember many things you've done wrong over the years. He told me my faults from years ago, and the problems I had caused other people. Here we were in this idyllic place, on pilgrimage to a holy site, and he went on and on, "You did this and you did that. So many people complain about you."

I'm usually very sensitive to criticism and easily hurt. So I determined, "I'm going to give all this pain to my self-cherishing attitude." I meditated like this as we were walking along, and much to my surprise, I started thinking, "This is good! I really welcome your criticism. I'm going to learn from it. Thank you for helping to consume my negative karma by telling me my faults. All the pain goes to my selfish attitude because that's my real enemy. Tell me more."

When we finally set up camp for the evening and made tea, my mind was completely peaceful. I think this was the blessing of the pilgrimage because it proved to me that it is possible to be happy when unwished-for things occur. I didn't have to fall into my old habit of "Poor me. Other people don't appreciate me."

Is It the Person's Nature to Be Disagreeable?

There's yet another technique to prevent anger when someone harms us. We ask ourselves, "Is it this person's nature to harm us?" If the person's nature is harmful and obnoxious, then getting angry at him is useless. It would be like getting angry at fire because its nature is to burn. That's just the way fire is; that's just the way this person is. Becoming upset about it is senseless.

Similarly, if the person's nature isn't harmful, then there's no use getting angry at him. His inconsiderate behavior was a fluke; it's not his nature. When it rains, we aren't mad at the sky, because the rain clouds aren't the nature of the sky.

In one way, we can say it's human nature to mistreat others upon occasion. We're all sentient beings caught in the net of cyclic existence, so of course our minds are obscured by ignorance, anger and attachment. If that's our present situation, then why expect ourselves or others to be free of misconceptions and disturbing attitudes? There's no reason to be angry at others because they cause harm, just as there's no reason to be angry at fire because it burns. That's just the way it is.

On the other hand, the deepest nature of even the most harmful people isn't harmful. They have the pure Buddha potential, their intrinsic goodness. This is their real nature. Their obnoxious behavior is like a thundercloud which temporarily obscures the clear sky. That behavior isn't them, so why make ourselves miserable by being impatient? Thinking this way is extremely helpful.

Holding Grudges

To transform our anger, we must apply these techniques to actual situations. In our daily meditation, we can pull out painful experiences from our memory and look at them in light of these techniques. We all have a reservoir of painful memories or grudges against others that we still hold. Instead of suppressing them, it's helpful to draw them out and use some of the above methods to reinterpret them. In this way, we'll be able to let go of lingering hurt and resentment.

If we don't do this, we find ourselves holding grudges for twenty or thirty years. We make ourselves miserable by carefully guarding these memories and never forgetting the harm we received. Families are very good at holding grudges. I know an extended family that purchased two houses for summer holidays on one piece of property. One day, the people in one house quarreled with their siblings and cousins in the other house, and since then they haven't spoken to each other. Over forty years ago, they decided they hated each other and wouldn't speak to each other for the rest of their lives. The families still go on holiday there, but they don't speak to each other. It's sad, isn't it?

Let's look at the grudges we've held for years: a small incident happens—someone didn't come to a wedding or a funeral, or embarrassed us in front of others—and we vow never to speak to or be nice to that person for as long as we live. We keep these kinds of vows perfectly, whereas we find it difficult not to transgress vows not to steal or lie.

If people harm us, instead of holding a grudge or seeking revenge, we can try to understand that the reason they harmed us was because they wanted happiness and to avoid pain. They may have used confused means for actualizing this, but in the context of their own suffering and confusion they were nevertheless seeking a way to be happy. This doesn't mean we whitewash or deny bad situations. Rather, we acknowledge them, but also go beyond getting stuck in our anger.

When we hold a grudge, our grudge neither harms the other person nor helps us. In fact, just the opposite occurs. The other person harmed us once or twice or some fixed number of times in the past. Yet each day when we remember the harm and become hurt or angry about it, we're harming ourselves again in the present. That's why we say that holding a grudge is an excellent form of self-torture. And if we do succeed in retaliating and causing them pain in return, don't we later have a hard time respecting ourselves? How can we feel dignity as human beings if we delight in deliberately harming others?

Someone may ask, "According to your previous comments, aren't we helping people purify their negative karma when we harm them in return?" No, not when our minds are belligerent and vengeful. The technique of considering receiving harm as a way of purifying negative karma is to be used to help us deal with harm that we can't stop. We must not invert it, rationalizing our own base intentions and harmful behavior by saying, "I'm helping others purify their negative karma."

It may take a while to free our minds from grudges that we've held for a long time. We must replace habitual anger with habitual patience, and this takes time and consistent effort. Of course, prevention is the best medicine. Rather that let our anger build up over time, it's better to be courageous and try to communicate with the other person early on. This stops the proliferation of misunderstandings. If we allow our anger to build up over time, how can we blame it on the other person? We have some responsibility to try to communicate with people who disturb us.

Nowadays, many people hold on to hurt received years ago and nurture anger toward those who harmed them. Yet, holding grudges serves no productive purpose. It eats at us, like mental cancer. As long as we hold onto our resentment, we can never forgive others, and our lack of forgiveness hurts no one but ourselves. To heal from our pain, there's no other alternative but to let go our anger and forgive others. Telling ourselves we *should* forgive others does no good; we must actively train ourselves to look at the situation from another viewpoint, which then allows us naturally to let go of the hurt and anger.

Why do we often find it so difficult to forgive others' mistakes? We too have made mistakes. Looking at our own behavior, we notice that sometimes we were overcome by disturbing attitudes and acted in ways that we later regretted. We want others to understand and forgive our mistakes—why then not let ourselves forgive others? Forgiving doesn't mean being naive, letting others manipulate us, or whitewashing problems. We can forgive an alcoholic for being drunk, but that doesn't mean we expect him or her to remain sober from now on. We can forgive a person for lying to us, but in the future, it may be wise to check his or her words. We can forgive a spouse for having an extramarital affair, but we shouldn't ignore the problems in the marriage that led our spouse to seek companionship elsewhere.

To have a free and open heart involves internal springcleaning; we must take out all our old grudges and look at the pain, but without rerunning the same self-pitying video in our minds. We can look at those situations from a fresh perspective by employing the various techniques for dissolving anger that have been described above. In this way, we'll let go of hostility that we've carried in our hearts for years. We'll also gain familiarity with the techniques so we can swiftly recall them when incidents occur in our daily lives.

Is the Other Person Happy?

One final technique for working with anger is to ask ourselves, "Is the person who is harming me happy?" Suppose someone shouts at us and complains about almost everything we do. Is she happy or miserable? Obviously, she's miserable. That's why she's acting this way. If she were happy, she wouldn't be quarrelsome.

We all know what it's like to be unhappy—that's exactly how the other person is feeling right now. Let's put ourselves in her shoes. When we're unhappy and "letting it all out," how would we like others to react? Generally, we want them to understand and help us. That's how the other person feels. So how can we be angry with her? She should be the object of our compassion, not our anger. If we think like this, we'll find our hearts filled with patience and loving-kindness for the other, no matter how she acts toward us. Our attitude will change, because instead of seeing the situation from our own self-centered viewpoint—what someone is doing to *me*—we'll put ourselves in the other person's shoes, experience her pain and feel her wish to be happy. Seeing that in essence she is just like us, it's easy to think, "How can I help her?" Such an attitude not only prevents us from becoming upset, but also inspires us to relieve the other person's misery.

How can we help someone who is creating negative karma by getting angry at us? Each situation is different and must be examined separately. However, some general guidelines may apply. First, pause, listen and consider whether others' complaints about us are justified. If so, we can apologize and correct the situation. That often stops their anger. Second, when people are upset and angry, try to calm them down. Don't argue back, because in their present state of mind, they won't be able to listen to you. This is understandable: we don't listen to others when we're in a temper. So, it's better to help them settle down and discuss it later.

When we discuss disagreements, it's better to listen attentively to others' feelings and complaints and to do what is called reflective or active listening. Here, we summarize how the situation appears in their eyes and their feelings about it and say this to them, without commenting on whether we agree with what they said. This allows us to check whether our interpretations of what they're thinking and feeling are accurate, and it also lets them know that we have understood what their feelings, needs and concerns are. Others relax when they feel that we understand what they're saying. Then, we tell them how the situation appears to us, how we feel and what our needs and concerns are. Dialogue can now ensue.

Anger at Ourselves

Sometimes we become angry at ourselves, going on an extensive tirade about how incompetent or unlovable we are. This often leads to depression and more self-hatred. While it's wise to recognize our mistakes and weaknesses, we needn't hate ourselves for having them. We're sentient beings, caught in cyclic existence due to our disturbing attitudes and karma, so of course we aren't perfect. We need to practice love and compassion toward ourselves as well. All beings have the potential to become fully enlightened Buddhas. It's important to recognize and appreciate that potential within ourselves. We can feel joyful that the path to enlightenment exists and that we can practice it. Rather than get angry at ourselves, we can regret our mistakes and purify them by means of the four opponent powers described earlier. By developing and purifying our minds in this way, we can become Buddhas. How can we hate a Buddha-to-be?

The Techniques in Brief

In conclusion, according to Buddhism, we're neither good nor bad when we're angry. The question is, "Does anger benefit us? Is it realistic?" Patience—a mental attitude that is calm and undisturbed in the face of harm and difficulty—is an alternative to either exploding with anger or repressing it. Patience gives us the clarity of mind to act appropriately and effectively. In addition, compassion for ourselves and others, for victims and perpetrators alike, can be a powerful motivator to act to remedy destructive situations. Several techniques to help dissolve our anger have been discussed. To review them:

1. Remember the example of someone saying we have a nose on our face or horns on our head. We can acknowledge our faults and mistakes, just as we acknowledge having a nose; there's no need to get angry when someone points out something that is obvious. On the other hand, if someone blames us for something we didn't do, it's as if he or she said

we have horns on our head. There's no reason to be angry at something that is untrue.

2. Ask ourselves, "Can I do something about it?" If we can, then anger is out of place because we can act to improve the situation. If we can't change the situation, anger is useless because there's no action we can take.

3. Examine how we got involved in the situation. This has two parts:

- What actions did we do recently to prompt the disagreement? Examining this helps us understand why the other person is upset.

- Recognize that unpleasant situations are due to our having harmed others earlier in this life or in previous lives. Seeing our own destructive actions as the principal cause, we can learn from past mistakes and resolve to act more wisely in the future.

4. Remember the benefit we can receive from an enemy. First, he or she points out our mistakes so we can correct them and improve our character. Second, he or she gives us the opportunity to practice patience, a necessary quality in our spiritual development. In these ways, the enemy is kinder to us that our friends or even the Buddha.

5. Give the pain to our selfish attitude by recognizing it is the source of all our problems.

6. Ask ourselves, "Is it the person's nature to act like this?" If it is, then there's no reason to be angry, for it would be like being annoyed with fire for burning. If it isn't the person's nature, again anger is unrealistic, for it would be like getting angry at the sky for having clouds in it.

7. Examine the disadvantages of anger and grudge-holding. This gives us tremendous energy to let go of these destructive emotions.

8. Recognize that the others' unhappiness and confusion cause them to harm us. Because we know what it's like to be unhappy, we can empathize with these people. Then they

become the objects of our compassion, rather than the objects of our anger.

Whether or not these techniques work for us depends on our effort. We have to practice them repeatedly to build up new mental and emotional habits. Keeping medicine in a drawer without taking it doesn't cure the illness. Similarly, just learning these antidotes without putting them into practice won't lessen our anger. Our peace of mind is our own responsibility.

GLOSSARY

Altruistic intention (bodhicitta): the mind dedicated to attaining enlightenment in order to benefit all others most effectively.

Arhat: a person who has attained liberation and is free from cyclic existence.

Bodhisattva: a person who has developed the spontaneous altruistic intention.

Buddha: any person who has purified all defilements and developed all good qualities. "The Buddha" refers to Shakyamuni Buddha, who lived 2,500 years ago in India.

Buddha nature (Buddha potential): the innate qualities of the mind enabling all beings to attain enlightenment.

Buddhist deity: a manifestation of the enlightened minds appearing in a physical form.

Compassion: the wish for all others to be free from suffering and its causes.

Concentration: the ability to remain single-pointedly on the object of meditation.

Cyclic existence (samsara): uncontrollably being reborn under the influence of disturbing attitudes and karmic imprints.

Determination to be free: the attitude aspiring to be free from all problems and sufferings and to attain liberation.

Dharma: our wisdom realizing emptiness, and the absence of suffering and its causes that this wisdom brings. In a more general sense, Dharma refers to the teachings and doctrine of the Buddha.

Disturbing attitudes: attitudes, such as ignorance, attachment, anger, pride, jealousy and closed-mindedness, that disturb our mental peace and propel us to act in ways harmful to others.

Empowerment (initiation): a ceremony in Vajrayana Buddhism in which the disciple is authorized to meditate on a particular manifestation of the Buddha.

Emptiness: the lack of independent or inherent existence. This is the ultimate nature or reality of all persons and phenomena.

Enlightenment (Buddhahood): the state of a Buddha, i.e. the state of having forever eliminated all obscurations from our mindstream, and having developed our good qualities and wisdom to their fullest extent. Buddhahood supersedes liberation.

Fantasized ways of existing: see inherent or independent existence.

Imprint: the residual energy left on the mindstream when an action has been completed. When it matures, it influences our experience. Imprints are also called karmic seeds.

Inherent or independent existence: a false and nonexistent quality that we project onto persons and phenomena; existence independent of causes and conditions, parts or the mind labeling a phenomena.

Initiation: see Empowerment.

Karma: intentional action. Our actions leave imprints on our mindstreams which bring about our experiences.

Liberation: freedom from cyclic existence.

Love: the wish for all others to have happiness and its causes.

Mahayana: the Buddhist tradition that asserts all beings can attain enlightenment. It strongly emphasizes the development of compassion and the altruistic intention.

Mantra: a series of syllables consecrated by a Buddha and expressing the essence of the entire path to enlightenment. They are recited to concentrate and purify the mind.

Meditation: habituating ourselves with positive attitudes and correct perspectives.

Mind: the experiential, cognitive part of living beings. Formless, the mind isn't made of atoms, nor is it perceivable through our five senses.

Mindstream: the continuity of the mind.

Monk: celibate male ordained practitioners.

Nirvana: the cessation of unsatisfactory conditions and their causes.

Nun: celibate female ordained practitioners.

Ordination: taking the precepts set out by the Buddha to restrain from destructive actions. There are various levels of ordination for both lay people and monks and nuns, but in general the term is used to refer to the precepts taken by monks and nuns.

Positive potential: imprints of positive actions, which will result in happiness in the future. Sometimes translated as "merit" or "good karma."

Precepts (vows): guidelines set out by the Buddha to help us refrain from destructive actions.

Priest: non-celibate Buddhist clergy from the various Japanese Buddhist traditions.

Pure Land: a Mahayana Buddhist tradition emphasizing methods to gain rebirth in a pure land. A pure land is a place established by a Buddha or bodhisattva where all conditions are conducive for the practice of Dharma and the attainment of enlightenment.

Realization: a clear, deep and correct understanding of what the Buddha taught. This may be either conceptual or nonconceptual direct experience. The non-conceptual direct realizations gained at higher levels of the path cleanse the obscurations from our minds forever.

Sangha: any person who directly and nonconceptually realizes emptiness. In a more general sense, sangha refers to the communities of ordained monks and nuns. It sometimes is used to refer to Buddhists in general.

Selflessness: see emptiness.

Special insight (vipassana): discriminating wisdom understanding the empty nature of phenomena.

Suffering (duhkha): any dissatisfactory condition. It doesn't refer only to physical or mental pain, but includes all problematic and unsatisfactory conditions.

Taking refuge: entrusting our spiritual development to the guidance of the Buddhas, Dharma and Sangha.

Tantra: a scripture describing the Vajrayana practice. This term can also refer to the Vajrayana practice itself.

Theravada: the Tradition of the Elders. A Buddhist tradition widespread in Southeast Asia and Sri Lanka.

Three Jewels: the Buddhas, Dharma and Sangha.

Vajrayana: a Mahayana Buddhist tradition popular in Tibet and Japan.

Vow: see Precepts.

Wisdom realizing reality (wisdom realizing emptiness, wisdom realizing the lack of fantasized ways of existing): an attitude that correctly understands the manner in which all persons and phenomena exist, i.e., the mind realizing the emptiness of inherent existence.

Zen (Ch'an): a Mahayana Buddhist tradition popular in China and Japan.

FUTHER READING

Dhammananda, K. Sri. *How to Live Without Fear and Worry.*
Buddhist Missionary Society; Kuala Lumpur, 1989.

Dhammananda, K. Sri. *What Buddhists Believe.* Buddhist Missionary Society; Kuala Lumpur, 1987.

Dhammananda, K. Sri, ed. *The Dhammapada.* Sasana Abhiwurdhi Wardhana Society; Kuala Lumpur, 1988.

Dharmaraksita. *The Wheel of Sharp Weapons.* Library of Tibetan Works and Archives; Dharamsala, India, 1981.

Eppsteiner, Fred, ed. *Path of Compassion.* Parallax; Berkeley, 1988.

Gampopa. *The Jewel Ornament of Liberation.* trans. by Herbert Guenther. Shambhala; Boulder, CO, 1971.

Goldstein, Joseph. *The Experience of Insight.* Shambhala; Boston, 1987.

Gyatso, Geshe Kelsang. *Meaningful to Behold.* Tharpa; London, 1986.

Hanh, Thich Nhat. *Being Peace.* Parallax; Berkeley, 1987.

H.H. Tenzin Gyatso, the 14th Dalai Lama. *The Dalai Lama at Harvard.* trans. by Jeffrey Hopkins. Snow Lion; Ithaca, NY, 1989.

Kapleau, Philip, ed. *The Three Pillars of Zen.* Rider; London, 1980.

Khema, Ayya. *Being Nobody, Going Nowhere.* Wisdom; Boston, 1987.

Kornfield, Jack and Brieter, Paul, eds. *A Still Forest Pool.* Theosophical Publishing House; Wheaton, IL, 1987.

Longchenpa. *Kindly Bent to Ease Us.* trans. by Herbert Guenther. Dharma; Emeryville, CA, 1978.

McDonald, Kathleen. *How to Meditate.* Wisdom; Boston, 1984.

Murcott, Susan. *The First Buddhist Women: Translations and Commentary on the* Therigatha. Parallax Press; Berkeley, 1991.

Nyanaponika, Thera. *Heart of Buddhist Meditation.* Rider; London, 1962.

Rabten, Geshe and Dhargyey, Geshe. *Advice from a Spiritual Friend.* Wisdom; Boston, 1986.

Rinpoche, Sogyal. *The Tibetan Book of Living and Dying.* Harper Collins; New York, 1992.

Rinpoche, Zopa. *Transforming Problems: Utilizing Happiness and Suffering in the Spiritual Path.* Wisdom; Boston, 1987.

Schumann, H.W. *The Historical Buddha.* Arkana; London, 1989.

Sparham, Gareth, trans. *Tibetan Dhammapada.* Wisdom; Boston, 1983.

Stevenson, Ian. *Cases of the Reincarnation Type.* 4 vols. University of Virginia Press; Charlottesville, 1975.

Story, Francis. *Rebirth as Doctrine and Experience.* Buddhist Publication Society; Kandy, Shri Lanka, 1975.

Suzuki, D.T. *An Introduction to Zen Buddhism.* Rider; London, 1969.

Suzuki, Shunriyu. *Zen Mind, Beginner's Mind.* Weatherhill; New York, 1980.

Trungpa, Chogyam. *Cutting Through Spiritual Materialism.* Shambhala; London, 1973.

Tsomo, Karma Lekshe, ed. *Sakyadhita: Daughters of the Buddha.* Snow Lion; Ithaca, NY, 1988.

Tsongkhapa, Je. *The Three Principal Aspects of the Path.* Mahayana Sutra and Tantra Press; Howell, NJ, 1988.

Wangchen, Geshe. *Awakening the Mind of Enlightenment.* Wisdom; Boston, 1988.

Willis, Janice D., ed. *Feminine Ground.* Snow Lion; Ithaca, NY, 1987.

Yeshe, Lama Thubten. *Introduction to Tantra.* Wisdom; Boston, 1987.

RESOURCES

The list below is not exhaustive of all the resources available. Each organization listed below should be able to put you in touch with similar organizations in your area.

For information on socially engaged Buddhism:

Buddhist Peace Fellowship, Box 4650, Berkeley CA 94704, U.S.A.

For information on women and Buddhism:

Sakyadhita (Daughters of the Buddha), 400 Hobron Lane #2615, Honolulu HI 96815, U.S.A.
NIBWA newsletter, c/o Dr. Chatsumarn Kabilsingh, Faculty of Liberal Arts, Thammat University, Bangkok 10200, Thailand

For Buddhist materials for children:

Department of Buddhist Education, Buddhist Churches of America, 1710 Octavia St., San Francisco CA 94109, U.S.A. (They produce the cartoon video, "The Life of the Buddha" in three parts and have Sunday School material.)
Dharma Press, 2425 Hillside Ave., Berkeley CA 94704, U.S.A.
Snow Lion Publications, Box 6483, Ithaca NY 14851, U.S.A.

For listings of Buddhist temples and centers:

Moreale, Don. *Buddhist America.* John Muir Publications; Santa Fe NM, 1988.

For inter-religious dialogue:

Council for a Parliament of the World's Religions, P.O. Box 1630, Chicago IL 60690-1630, U.S.A.

American Buddhist Congress, 933 S. New Hampshire Ave., Los Angeles CA 90006, U.S.A.